THE THIRTY-DAY CHALLENGE TO

Fall in Love

WITH THE MAN OF YOUR DREAMS

An engaging journey
into the banquet house of the Lord for
single, divorced, and widowed
women of God

Based on the Song of Solomon

Now, every woman of God can heal her life
and position herself for healthy, godly love
in just thirty days!

TONI EUBANKS

Trilogy Christian Publishers
A Wholly Owned Subsidiary of Trinity Broadcasting Network
2442 Michelle Drive, Tustin, CA 92780

Copyright © 2021 by Toni Eubanks

All Scripture quotations, unless otherwise noted, taken from THE HOLY BIBLE, NEW INTERNATIONAL VERSION®, NIV® Copyright © 1973, 1978, 1984, 2011 by Biblica, Inc.® Used by permission. All rights reserved worldwide.

Scripture quotations marked (KJV) taken from The Holy Bible, King James Version. Cambridge Edition: 1769.

Scripture quotations marked (AMPC) taken from Amplified Bible, Classic Edition. The "Amplified" trademark is registered in the United States Patent and Trademark Office by The Lockman Foundation. All rights reserved.

All Scripture marked with the designation (GW) is taken from GOD'S WORD®. © 1995, 2003, 2013, 2014, 2019, 2020 by God's Word to the Nations Mission Society. Used by permission.

For information, address Trilogy Christian Publishing Rights Department, 2442 Michelle Drive, Tustin, CA 92780.

Trilogy Christian Publishing/ TBN and colophon are trademarks of Trinity Broadcasting Network.

For information about special discounts for bulk purchases, please contact Trilogy Christian Publishing.

Manufactured in the United States of America

Trilogy Disclaimer: The views and content expressed in this book are those of the author and may not necessarily reflect the views and doctrine of Trilogy Christian Publishing or the Trinity Broadcasting Network.

10 9 8 7 6 5 4 3 2 1
Library of Congress Cataloging-in-Publication Data is available.
ISBN 978-1-64773-500-5
ISBN 978-1-64773-501-2 (ebook)

DEDICATION

To my daughters, Tara and Trina, the catalysts in my life that God has used repeatedly to help me remain focused and steadfast in prayer and obedience: thank you for your love, your support, and for being the women of God that He has called you to be. May your lives always be led by His grace, His mercy, and His power. I love you more than words can express.

To my husband, Karl: you are the one I have needed for so long. I thank God for His timing for our love story. You are my sweetheart forever. I love you now and always.

To my mother, Elizabeth: you supported me since childhood, holding me close to you and in prayer for years until God was ready to reveal Himself in me. I love you eternally.

To my brother, Tim: you have been the wind beneath my wings so many times that I cannot count them. I am forever grateful to God for planting us in the same family. I love you forever.

Lastly, to every woman of God who has ever been hurt or abused: come and dine with me at my Father's house where there is bread enough to spare.

FOREWORD

A revolution of healing has come. So, put on your seat belt, ladies, because this is a ride you will not forget! *The Thirty-Day Challenge to Connect and Fall in Love with the Man of Your Dreams* includes a thirty-day healing "love calendar" that uproots inner hurts skillfully and privately. The book takes women of God on a supernatural rendezvous with Beloved, the King of kings and the Lord of lords. Not only does the book prepare the heart to experience emotional healing, but it also walks women of God step-by-step through the emotional healing process, digging up and removing their hindrances as they read the book and do the work. Toni propels women into the secret place in the stairs as mentioned in the Song of Solomon and she even allows them to fall in love there with Beloved. The lessons taught in this book are lessons of purpose and power that will securely move Christian women into the destiny that God has planned for them, regardless of their situation. This is a book that has long been needed in the body of Christ. Daughters of Zion, you have not been forgotten. *The Thirty-Day Challenge to Connect and Fall in Love with the Man of Your Dreams* will remove the pain of your past, lead you to victory, then cause you to soar!

—Bishop Josephine Smith,
Rehoboth Ministry,
Houston, Texas

ACKNOWLEDGMENT

James Everson III was the wisest man I have ever known in the earthly realm. He led me through troubled waters more than a few times, and I led him to Jesus Christ. I am sure he is with Father God rejoicing that this work has come to fruition. How's the view, Jimmy?

SPECIAL ACKNOWLEDGMENT

None have touched my soul like Barbara Brown-Hardman. You saw me when no one else did and validated me. Best friends for life!

INTRODUCTION

It seems that every major revival and move of God, whether it starts in our hearts, our churches, or our communities, first begins in 2 Chronicles 7:14 (KJV):

> "If my people, which are called by my name, shall humble themselves, and pray, and seek my face, and turn from their wicked ways; then will I hear from heaven, and will forgive their sin, and will heal their land."

There is an individual revival of fire that is growing in each of us. It is a rising hunger to know Him. This desire is comprehensible to everyone. He is lighting us and making Himself known because the night will get darker. So, do not miss your visitation. You are troubled because you need Him. Do not ignore this time. It is not about the crowds, pseudo beliefs, or keeping up with others; it is about Him.

The world is going to hell in a handbasket fast. It is time to enter in before you get left out. No more playing games, no more pretending. God is serious. The devil is serious, too, but God is serious about you: about your life and about your heart.

Lay it down. Put it all aside, seek Him, and come in. Get secured. Remove all desperation, desperate acts, and desperate decisions, because He is revealing Himself and He will burn whatever He did not plant out with the fire of His presence. It is time to advance the kingdom of God within us. Ready, set, God.

TABLE OF CONTENTS

Dedication iii
Foreword v
Acknowledgement. vii
Special Acknowledgement. ix
Introduction xi

Prologue 1
Part 1: Seeing Him 3
Part 2: The Gospel of Peace 31
Part 3: Women on Fire 43
Part 4: The Cost 63
Part 5: Extracting Gold 79
Part 6: It's Time. 91

The Thirty-Day Love Challenge Calendar. 93
Measuring Your Heart 95
Introduction 101
The Challenge 105
   Day 1 106
   Day 2 108
   Day 3 110
   Day 4 114
   Day 5 116
   Day 6 118
   Day 7 120
   Day 8 122
   Day 9 124
   Day 10 126

Day 11 128
Day 12 130
Day 13 132
Day 14 134
Day 15 136
Day 16 138
Day 17 140
Day 18 142
Day 19 144
Day 20 146
Day 21 148
Day 22 150
Day 23 152
Day 24 154
Day 25 156
Day 26 158
Day 27 160
Day 28 162
Day 29 164
Day 30 166
Your New Beginning Starts Here 169
Prayer of Salvation 181

About the Author 183
Scripture Appendix 185

PROLOGUE

God wants you to experience firsthand the overwhelming, never-ending, reckless love that He has for you. It is a love so amazing that it will go to whatever length needed, whatever depth required to bring you back to Him; a love so radical it will slay every enemy, destroy every form of wickedness, and even set darkness on fire. If you made your bed in hell, His love would rescue you and bring you back to Him. Death could not hold Him; it even bowed before Him. His love chases after you. There is no mountain too high, no valley too low. His love is faithfully searching until you are found. You cost Him everything; now, He will stop at nothing. His love is coming after you. It is the overwhelming, never-ending, reckless love of God.

The Thirty-Day Challenge to Connect and Fall in Love with the Man of Your Dreams will prepare you for God's remarkable love, then usher you into the very presence of love Himself. It was especially written for every single, divorced, and widowed woman of God, but it was also written for every woman of God who has found herself in a challenging and love-deficient marriage. Healing your life and experiencing God's love will make a difference in your walk with the Lord. Meet Beloved and learn how to progressively become more deeply and intimately acquainted with the wonders of His person. There, you will fall in love the right way. Now, every Christian woman can remove the pain of her past and heal and restore her life in just thirty days. Your emotional wholeness will automatically reposition you for healthy and godly love. Get ready to meet your own intended destiny.

PART 1: SEEING HIM

Who Is He?

Has someone ever caught your eye, causing you to think to yourself, Who is that? Did their presence draw you? Could you not get them off your mind? Well, that is how I feel about my love relationship with the Lord Jesus Christ. I cannot get enough of Him. I cannot get Him off my mind. I am taken, obsessed, and enamored by Him. He draws me! The Bible says in the Song of Solomon that His love is better than wine. He takes my breath away and I am genuinely ravished by Him.

He Sustains Me

Hello, I'm evangelist Toni Eubanks, and I want to take you on a life-changing, destiny-altering journey with myself and with the Lord Jesus Christ. I'm excited about this emotional and healing journey that we're about to embark upon because this voyage is going to bring you to a place in God that will cause you to know Him so deeply that when the storms come and the winds of life blow, you will remain steadfast and affixed to Him with unbroken fellowship underneath His everlasting arms. So, receive from the outflow of His resurrection, and regardless of whether you are single, divorced, widowed, in a troubled marriage, or you simply desire a closer walk with the Lord, this journey will give you the tools necessary to sustain you emotionally and to fill you with joy and contentment throughout the tempests of life.

This coming expedition will produce an intimate encounter with the Lord Jesus Christ in a way you have never experienced before. This trek has a destination that will lead you to His breathtaking banquet table: the same table discovered by the woman in the Song of Solomon. You will visit Beloved there and experience a lasting spiritual satisfaction as she did. It is a rendezvous of delight that leads to the secret place of the stairs where the Lord of your salvation will also become the Lover of your heart and soul.

Afterwards, whenever you meditate or think about Him, there will be a spiritual mealtime that will automatically be provided within. In the secret place, He will uncover your visage in Him, and there, your voice will be heard by Him; there, you will become a garden enclosed just for Him so that in the face of difficult and troubled times, His peace will rise from deep within you and garrison your heart. You will be able to automatically tap into a love spring that will feed your spirit with an unceasing sense of wholeness and peace. This lasting meal I am speaking of is located at His banquet table, the place where your delights will be fulfilled. However, there is a journey that we must first take; a trek we must make that will prepare our hearts to meet Him.

Spiritual Focus Brings Rewards

Although this journey will require and demand spiritual focus from you, it offers benefits, delights, and spiritual encounters as your reward. These encounters will become a wellspring of peace as you continue to walk through life. You will search within your own spirit and find that there is something that preserves you emotionally; that there is something keeping you from the pitfalls where others, even other believers, are finding themselves. That love relationship and unbroken connection to His table will become an overflowing and sustaining source inside you. It will create an affair of the heart that will never end. I know because I have been benefiting from the meals from His banquet table for many years; my wholeness is not established in another person or in things, but in my connection to Christ, the Lover of my soul. That intimate connection frees me to worship, to serve, and to enjoy life.

This connection belongs to all who know Christ and name Him as Lord, but these special provisions are only appropriated if we are willing to take the journey that leads us to the secret place provided for us. It is a place where we can sit and dine with Him, consume His delights, and open the gifts provided for us on His behalf. Then, we can adorn ourselves with His delights and utilize them in our lives.

Ladies, this is a five-part series that precedes a thirty-day challenge for Christian women to connect and fall in love. This thirty-day challenge will bring you peace and spiritual intimacy with the Lord Jesus Christ on a level that you have never experienced before. You will finally come to know Him as the Lover of your soul. The Challenge will prepare you for destiny, satisfy your longing heart, and give you a spiritual "glow" of love that only lovers share. This encounter will sanctify your heart and even prepare you for a natural love. In other words, God wants to heal your life and clear the path for the man of God that He has chosen for you. In short, this thirty-day challenge is a set up for your own blessing.

The Song of Solomon is a spiritual depiction of the love affair between Jesus and the church, His body. However, for women of God—single, divorced, widowed, or those in love-deficient marriages—there is preservation within the verses that offers a thorough expression of a continuous and durable love interaction that the Lord desires to have with us right now. Hey, you— woman of God! God wants intimacy with you, now! Yes, He wants intimacy with you and He's calling your name right now! So, do you want the blessing of God? Well, you must first tap into Him. I used to say all the time, "I want to be under the spout where the glory's coming out!" What about you?

You see, the blessing is not just waiting for you to get to heaven. You will not need it there. The blessing is not waiting for

Jesus' triumphant return to overtake you. You will not need it then, either. No. The blessing of the Lord is available for you right now, and if you are married, do not think you have to wait for your husband to have a sudden epiphany, begin to see what you need, and miraculously start loving you just the right way so that it will heal your heart and make you whole. He's not supernatural; after all, he is just a man, but Jesus, your awaiting Lover, desires to whisper to you all the things your heart desires to hear. He not only wants to calm you and plant His peace within you, but He also wants to cause you to beam with His presence and give you a glow that only lovers share. Yes, my sister! Jesus wants you to glow!

Glow, Glow, Glow!

Okay. So, just what is this "glow"? Well, you have probably seen the glow and did not even know you were seeing it. You saw the glow when you looked at a woman who was expecting a baby. She first started glowing at a time when she did not even know she was pregnant, but because she was pregnant, the glow showed up even though she was not yet aware that her baby was on the way. The glow knew it, so it showed up, announcing that which was hidden inside her. Others can tell; they could see that she was pregnant before she was even aware that there was a baby on board. You also see it at times when a person falls in love; they get the glow, too. Do you remember seeing someone who had just recently fallen in love and you just knew there was something different and profound about them even though they had not yet mentioned their fresh, new love? Anyone could have prophesied their joy because they were simply beaming from the inside out with their newfound love's presence. Their glow became visible.

In that same way, there is a "glow" waiting for you at the banquet table of the Lord. That is where you will receive His glow. When you enter the banquet room of the Lord, partake of His delights, and consume the spiritual meal prepared there by Him for you, you will radiate. Your newfound love relationship with Him will develop a glow in you that will grow until it produces a beaming light from your heart that becomes visible to others. You will become pregnant with His presence and His glow. His glow will announce what is inside you and display your relationship with Him for all to see. Others will be attracted to it. Some will openly bear witness, telling you that there is something special and different about you, even though they will not be able to exactly put their finger on what that amazing "something" is in you that has marked this difference. I know because I have had many people come up to me and say, "Are you aware that you are glowing?" My response: "Yes, yes I am." His glow makes you spiritually whole and even naturally attractive. His glow is essential to having an abundant lifestyle. This overflow will soothe your soul continually and keep your heart healed and whole. God wants to give you His glow.

Now, I know you thought you had to wait until you got married to a natural man to start glowing. Well, let me tell you something: you can get that glow right now from the Lord; it is a rich overflow that brings contentment to your life. The glow makes you beautifully attractive and it even draws people to you. This loving experience will position you for what God has for your future and it will even catapult you into your own intended destiny. It is truly amazing. People will look at you and think, I want what she's got!

I have often heard women say out loud, "Why is sister Toni always so blessed?" Well, listen carefully my sister: the secret is in the stairs of heaven! I want to teach you how to reach Him; how to ascend the stairs of heaven, how to ascend to the banquet room of the Lord in order to get everything you need to successfully walk out your life with Him. The secret is in intimacy with Him; not figuratively, but a literal intimacy with Him. That closeness is born out of time spent with God and spiritual encounters with the Prince of peace of my heart. His soothing touch renews me, His calming voice leads me, and His guiding light directs me. One intimate encounter with Him—the Lord of your heart—will change you forever.

Just like Queen Esther, you are the Lord's queen. When the queen is paired with her King, she walks throughout the land with His favor upon her. Wherever she goes, a light is upon her. She is favored by the King, so she is favored by all under the King. She is bound to Him, attached to her Beloved, and His lingering presence remains with her wherever she goes. She is special, and none can resist the visible magnetic anointing upon her, as it is the King's presence, abiding with her wherever she goes.

How would you like it if when you walked into a room, everybody took notice because you were chosen and there was a "glow" on you? Your connection with Beloved will create a permanent link between you and the Lover of your soul. You will not have to manufacture this glow; you will not have to try to make it manifest and work for you. It will simply happen, without your assistance, and it will happen just because you have spent time with Him at His table.

People will see God on you when you walk in the room, and God on you looks attractive. He brings favor upon your life and draws good things towards you, but most of all, He simply feels good resting on you and on your life! The glow is His presence abiding with and on you. The glow will even open doors for you. This is what you need; this is what is too often missing in the lives of women of God. Without it, they begin desperately seeking something to fill His void. However, no man is big enough to fill His place and give you what you need. God's glow removes your longings. God's presence on you brings peace and a calm assurance. This is the love that awaits you on this journey.

Although this challenge is made available to you, you must still choose to accept it and take the encounter seriously to get the full benefits that it offers. So, if you are single, divorced, widowed, in a love deficient-marriage, or simply desire a closer walk with the Lord, this is your opportunity to make the connection that will completely satisfy. Many women of God find themselves searching in the trash piles of the world because they have nothing to sustain them and no direction to lead them. Many end up shipwrecked and in broken and abusive relationships because they could not hear the voice of God whispering four important words: "He's not the one." God wants you sustained, He wants you preserved, and He wants you protected and provided for while He is positioning you for your destiny.

How Do You Truly See Yourself?

Changing the way you see yourself will change the way you feel. It will also ultimately change who you are drawn to and who is drawn to you. If you are hurting inside and you see yourself as unable, unbecoming, undeserving, or inadequate, you will feel hurt, insecure, and undeserving. You will draw the type of man that fits the way you feel about yourself, because as a man or woman thinketh in his or her heart, so is he or she. If you are broken inside, you will be drawn to, accept, and even go after broken men. I have said many times, "You can take a woman with a broken heart, put her in a place filled with all different kinds of men, and she will spot the broken one a mile away and mistake him for love every single time."

However, when you learn to care for your soul and take the time to heal your life, you begin to see your life through the lens of wholeness, and you lose your taste for broken men. Your heart stops hurting from the past. You realize that you are indeed a daughter of the King. You can sense your wholeness springing up from deep inside you. You become able, furnished, and fit. You can feel your secure attachment to your Beloved. Even during times of conflict, a calm assurance will rise and quietly take charge of the wheel of your life as you safely rest in Him because you know that He's got you.

You Belong

It is a wonderful feeling to know there is something special going on between you and the God of heaven and earth. Realizing that you are included in the greatness of His master plan is very stimulating. It creates the feeling of belonging; you know that God is with you. You are etched in His palm, you are a part of His forever plans, and you are on His mind. That awareness is electrifying. When you feel that way, you will not accept or attach yourself to just any Tom, Dick, or Harry that comes along. Because you've got so much going on between you and the Lord of the universe, you simply refuse to allow just any old "scrub" to interrupt what you and the Lord have between you.

Meeting the Lord in the clefts of the rock in the secret places of the stairs will help you reach those unchartered places within your own heart. These are the places that need Him; He will convert them to wholeness without you hardly noticing the conversion is taking place, that is until a challenge appears and you are now immediately able to stand, whereas you could not before. Ungodly distractions and no-good men will no longer have a hold on your heart or in your life. Your inner heart will rise in confidence because it knows that your Father knows what is best for you, and without hesitation, you will let Him lead. You will finally transition into the royalty that He created you to be, and just like Esther, you will become ready for the King. You will be prepared for life's journey because you have entered into the manifestation of His righteousness activated within you. You will walk as a part of His righteous lineage and He will adorn you for His purpose. You will feel your right standing in Him, and instead of wondering why someone else is always getting blessed, you will realize that you are the blessed one.

I want you to say out loud: "I am the blessed one!"

Say it again: "I am the blessed one!"

Get used to saying it, because you are indeed the blessed one.

Get Connected!

Ascending to the secret place with Him will allow you to always know and feel that you are blessed above measure, and once you learn how to get there, you can ascend to Him anytime you want. The Bible says that we are to be self-sufficient, requiring no aid or support. God wants you to feel sufficient in Him, but you can only maintain His sufficiency by maintaining your connection to Him. God made women fearfully and wonderfully unique and He understands us better than anyone. Our inner parts cry out to be filled and made whole by Him and Him alone.

Oftentimes, we attempt to enhance our beauty and get what we need from television, plastic surgery, makeup, and clothes, but those things can never truly fulfill us. The Word of God says beauty is vain and momentary, fleeting. If you do not know that yet, just keep right on living. Of course, I believe in looking and dressing well. I believe that God's daughters are supposed to look good, but who we are should not be wrapped up in how we look or what we wear. The Bible says to let it be the hidden man of the heart, even the ornament of a meek and quiet spirit that is attractive to God. God calls that woman valuable. That woman is at peace, not moved by anything that comes. She is confident and enclosed just for Him. He is her resting place and God is looking for her; He wants to answer her prayers.

We must attach ourselves to Him to really be secure. Because what we truly need can only come from Him, we must become His dovetail, fastened and secure, connected and harmonized to him. God wants you clasped to Him; only then will He dress you for your future and prepare you for your destiny.

The Lord's Dovetail

The Bible says that God saves our tears. We are precious to Him and uniquely made for a purpose. He is attracted to you and your very cry echoes His name and pulls Him towards you. He simply cannot get enough of you. Even the very words you are reading are a part of God drawing you. He knows you are hurting and tired of what you keep getting in life. He does not want you living your life with a deficit of love. He does not want you left out and lonely. It is God's desire that you feel complete and whole. He has an overflow that will fill your love-tank so you will never be thirsty that way again. This is what Jesus told the woman at the well in John 4:14. He told her that He would give her living water that would cause her to thirst no more, that it would be everlasting, and that she would not need to go to a well to draw it out. Too many women of God are going to the world's wells for water. However, because this woman was wise, she took Jesus up on His offer. She accepted the invitation from Jesus, and it changed her life forever!

The work God wants to do in your life, woman of God, will become a constant well, springing up inside you daily. It will totally enrich your life. Let's look at three different versions of the same verse found in Proverbs. Proverbs 10:22 (KJV) says:

> The blessing of the Lord, it maketh rich, and he addeth not sorrow with it.

Proverbs 10:22 (AMPC) says:

> The blessing of the Lord, it makes [truly] rich, and He adds no sorrow with it, neither does toiling increase it.

Proverbs 10:22 (NIV) says:

> The blessing of the Lord brings wealth, and he adds no trouble to it.

Whichever way you slice this verse, God is saying He wants your life filled to the brim with His goodness that satisfies.

A Broken "Chooser"

Many of us have gotten into relationships that in the beginning did not seem so bad. Initially, we were happy and excited, but then the relationship became problematic and yielded rotten and unproductive fruit. When we looked back at it, we realized that we did not use wisdom from the onset. We just wanted someone to call our own special "someone". We did not see the curve ball being thrown by the adversary to unravel and break the precious things in our lives. We got caught up in our emotions; we fell in love with being in love. So, we could not see all the coming trouble, that looking back should have been obvious until it was too late. By then, we were too far in to back up. To avoid shame and failure, we often work hard to try to make these relationships work, that is, until we are exhausted and have no choice but to leave them.

Problematic relationships do not end well. Far too many women of God are embedded in toxicity and unable to enter the destiny that God has ordained for them, because when the relationship is bad, it keeps you from advancing and moving forward. You become so busy nursing the relationship and putting out fires to keep it together that you can never get anything done or accomplished with the person. Something is always off, no matter what you do or how hard you try.

Consequently, many women of God spend years of their lives never advancing because of bad choices for relationships that were sent by Satan. Many are too proud, too ashamed, or too hardheaded to get out while they can. Shipwrecked, they remain unproductive for God, their children, and themselves. They live in mediocrity, often telling themselves many things to make them feel okay with what they know deep down is an ungodly union. Some women blame themselves for every negative thing that has happened, or they judge and blame the other person. However, no matter who is to blame, you still chose to say, "I do," to that joker, right? So, you are still a huge part of the blame. The buck must stop somewhere so that we can do better, because regardless to what he has done, you still married him.

Often, our "choosers" are broken. In other words, that little thing in your heart that told you that he was "the one" is broken. However, many of us are unaware that our "choosers" are often shattered in our young years. Often, because our inner issues first began with our family of origin, healing must be done in our hearts in those areas so that we can become completely whole. God wants to remove the shame and extinguish the pain in your life. Whether it be the shame that you have internalized against yourself or the hurt you have experienced from the hands of those who raised you, all must be taken to the Father to be healed.

You might be thinking, A lot has happened, and you do not know what they did to me. You do not know how I was treated by them, by him, on my job, or as a child. We often judge and feel entitled to feel and react the way we do because of the pain that others have caused us. However, the Bible says that if we judge, we will be judged. The key to a better life is learning how to heal the heart from the judgements we have made. Even though our hearts are reacting by hurting from what has happened, we must choose to forgive them anyway.

Through forgiveness, the heart becomes soothed, and over time, forgets the wounds inflicted upon it, allowing for healing to come. It does not matter if it happened years ago. Some wounds can run so deep and remain so fresh within our hearts that it is as though they happened ten minutes ago even though the inflicted wound may be ten years old or more. Emotional healing is essential to living the abundant life that Christ promised you in His Word.

Now, I am not belittling the severity of what has happened or the gravity of the things you have gone through, far from that. You see, I understand abuse because I have travelled through the valley of abuse, hurt, and toxicity, and I know the painful scars they leave to seep and linger in your life. So, I am not speaking outside of the pain of abuse. Rather, I am speaking from the mountaintop of healing, wholeness, and restoration. I am speaking from the place of abundance and all that God still wants to bring to pass for you, despite what has happened.

Defeating the Enemy

God not only wants to remove the pain of what has happened, but also to remove the brokenness it has produced in your life. When there is brokenness within, you can feel it long after the wound has been inflicted. Every time you think about what happened, it hurts, you become emotional or angry, and often bitterness will set in as well. Father God wants the power of the enemy defeated in your life so that your past is no longer a stumbling block that interferes with your future. He desires to pluck the very judgements you have made from your heart so that the heart can forget the pain of the past, be strengthened, and made whole. He wants to blanket you with favor and dress you for your destiny in the secret place where nothing can stop your rising.

You may be wondering, How can He dress and prepare me for my destiny if He is not interacting with me? God wants to bring you into His banquet house, a place where you can sup together. There He will prepare you for your own intended destiny. There, and there alone, He will reveal to you the intimacies of His connection to you so that when He advances you, you will live within His assurance.

The Marriage Feast

In Matthew 22:2-14 (KJV), Jesus tells a parable about a wedding feast and a king who instructed his servants to summon and invite all the people in the land to the wedding of his son. Excitedly, the people came from everywhere and every land. I am sure that just to get an invite from the king had to have been a huge honor for the common people. Eagerly, the large crowd of people all gathered to attend the amazing wedding of the king's son. The house was filled with guests and the wedding was furnished. However, one of the guests was not properly dressed for the event. Because he had chosen not to prepare himself, he was cast out of the affair. While others feasted, he was not able to enjoy what had been freely made available to him because his heart was not right.

All he had to do was get himself together and prepare for the wedding. The provisions had already been made for him and the invitations had been freely given, so it cost him nothing, but he operated from an evil heart and didn't think enough about the king's offer to prepare himself to enter into what had been provided. He was ungrateful and he showed the king how he truly felt by how he chose to dishonor him. His out-of-place attire was a reflection on the king, his family, and everyone who came properly dressed. I am sure he must have stood out as a spectacle, derailing the event. The king had no choice but to remove the show to preserve the purpose of the event.

The parable ends when Jesus states in Matthew 22:14 (KJV), "For many are called, but few are chosen." I like to say, "Many are called, but few choose to go to the trouble to prepare themselves for their calling." God loves you so much that He does not want to leave you as you are. He does not want your present state to hinder your future, but you do have a choice, and He will not make it for you.

Whispers from the Secret Place

Because of what they have been through, many women of God are not ready to meet the destiny God has planned for them. So, consequently, they remain shut out from it. However, Jesus wants to bring you into His banqueting house, remove your hindrances, and reposition you for what He has for you. Then, as you continue to do life, day in and day out, your inner glow will grow in intensity as you are being led by His Spirit into the plans He has for you. When you meet people who are not what they appear to be, you will find yourself walking away from them without hesitation because those old wineskins no longer have drawing power over your new wine. You have simply lost your taste for them, so your new wine remains preserved. Your relationship with Him will become an affair of the heart.

In the secret place in the stairs, He will whisper mysteries of His love to you. Yes, God has some things He wants to whisper to you, but there is so much in the way that interferes, so don't misinterpret your inability to hear Him for an unwillingness on His part to speak. God is always speaking to our hearts, but too often we are too weighted with cares, hurts, and wounds to hear Him. He has a purpose for you and He wants to remove all the interferences.

Remember that because He chose you, He had something that he chose you for. This means that He has something that He wants to impart inside your spirit, because there is something amazing that He has planned for you. There is a communication that must transpire between you and Him in order for Him to plant His plans within you. I call them "the whispers of God". When He whispers, we become steadfast and unmovable. It is a part of how He must dress our hearts for longevity and purpose. He wants to adorn you for good success. The Word of God says in Jeremiah 29:11 (AMPC), "For I know the thoughts and plans that I have for you, says the Lord, thoughts and plans for welfare and peace, and not for evil, to give you hope in your final outcome." You see, God has plans for you, but the devil has plans for you as well. The enemy of your soul wants you to go through life filled with unfulfilled promises, but God has so much more.

Know Your Own Destiny

Do you know what God has purposed for your life? If you are seeking God in this area, if you desire to see the promises of God fulfilled in your life, this book is for you. God has placed this book in your hands specifically to meet your need, to position you for your future, and to remove your hindrances. No, you did not just discover this book by chance. God heard your heart's cry; He saw your desire and He wants to change things in your life right now. Isn't it exciting to know that God truly has plans for us? Let Him transform you by His Spirit, because He is good.

Say a quick prayer with me out loud to God: "Lord, I am ready for You to reveal Yourself to me. I am ready to know You intimately and walk into what You have planned for my life, in Jesus' name. Amen."

A Big Plan is on the Horizon for You!

God truly has big plans for us, and yes, He is ready and willing to make them known to us. Jeremiah 29:11 (NIV) says, "'For I know the plans I have for you,' declares the Lord, 'plans to prosper you and not to harm you, plans to give you hope and a future.'" So, if you are in a relationship, and that relationship is producing physical or emotional harm to you, that relationship is not from God. God desires to give you a hope and a future. Do you feel as though you have a hope and a future, or are you just hoping and praying that things will just work themselves out? Are you closing your eyes spiritually and merely wishing for the best?

God has a hope and a future for you if you will only follow Him and believe. Jeremiah 29:12 (AMP) says, "Then you will call upon Me, and you will come and pray to Me, and I will hear and heed you." God is saying, "I want you to come." Are you willing to take this journey? Are you willing to take this challenge?

Salvation is Free, But Everything Else Has a Cost

The Lord wants you to come to Him. When you cry out to Him, He will listen to you, and when you seek for Him, He will show up. So many of us do not want to take the time to seek God, so we find ourselves lacking internally. I used to tell my girls when they were faced with a challenging course in school, dreading a test, performing in a recital, or competing in a sport, that along with prayer, they only needed to prepare and show up, that the rest is in God's hands, and that He would show up to help them—and He did. It is up to you to prepare and show up; God is waiting for you to do your part.

Are you ready to come out of captivity? If so, prepare to seek the Lord. When you realize that God is a necessity to your continual survival, seeking Him is no longer a dread; it becomes a pleasure. When Christian women try to cover their loneliness by trying to find the love of their lives themselves without healing and without Him, it leads to sadness. Many believe they will never find "Mr. Right", so they choose instead to settle for "Mr. Right Now", irrespective to what it might be producing in their lives and in their children's lives.

The Secret Place

> He brought me to the banqueting house, and his banner over me was love [for love waved as a protecting and comforting banner over my head when I was near him].
> —Song of Solomon 2:4 (AMPC)

Wow! God wants you near Him so that He can protect and comfort you from the top of your head to the bottom of your feet. I believe that in Song of Solomon 2:4, the Lord began to wave His banner over the woman's head first because he understands that women are often battling with their emotions and are fearful in their minds. We often torture ourselves with worries and fears even though the Word of God commands us to fear not, because Jesus is our solution. He wants you to feel the waving of His protection and comfort so that no matter what you face, you will always know that you are well cared for by Him.

So, let's do a spiritual exercise right here. Close your eyes: Imagine it is a super-hot summer day and you are sitting under a big, beautiful oak tree in the shade. Your eyes are shut, and suddenly you feel a nice, cool breeze gently whistling and flowing through the leaves of the tree, softly stroking your face. You can feel the relief of the breeze as you are slowly being restored from your head to your toes. Just stay there in the moment for a while. God's inner healing feels a lot like that.

The King of glory is in pursuit of you! His words are softly spoken, saying to come unto Him and find rest for your soul. Are you weary? Would you like to live within a calm assurance, to dwell within your very own place of peace? By faith, when you enter the truth that His banner is waving over you, you gain access to that reality through the power of His Word. This is when you activate the power, the protection, and the comfort available in that special place. That is when you begin living within its tangible manifestation as you feel the spiritual breeze of His love banner's wave. As it begins to produce in your life, you become one of the untouchable ones, protected and kept by Him. No, I am not saying the enemy will just pack his bags, go home, and never bother you again, but what I am saying is that the greater One will rise within you in a way that you have never experienced as you face obstacles.

His amazing presence will continually be with you leading you and guiding you. You will live within the experiential reality in which no weapon formed against you shall prosper and nothing can defeat your righteous cause. God wants to provide you His shield for your life more than you desire to have it. The Word of God declares, "Christ in you, the hope of glory." (Colossians 1:27, NIV). He wants to rise inside you and reveal His manifested glory through you and in your life. He wants to be the King of your heart. He wants to reveal Himself to you in a new and living way. Let Him whisper mysteries designed only for you concerning His plans for your life.

Get Into Expectation!

I praise God for His power, His awesome, awesome power! His ability to do work in us even in the middle of our mess is utterly amazing. However, there is work we must do to prepare to rendezvous with the Lord of hosts and the Prince of peace of our hearts, so there are preparations necessary to take this journey to His banquet house. There is no "gimme", or rather, no "freebie". You must be willing to do the work.

This generation always wants things instantaneously. We want results right away, "pronto", at the snap of our fingers, or at the press of our keyboard. We want what we want, and we want it now! We have become conditioned to not commit to anything that takes more than five minutes to complete. When we accept that type of mentality concerning our wholeness and our future, we position ourselves for emotional failure. Your healing is precious, and it requires time spent with Him. Your wholeness is worth more than a five-minute, half-baked hope and prayer.

God desires a genuine relationship with you. He needs you to surrender and give Him the time necessary to prepare you for your destiny. He needs time to transfer what you need inside your heart so that you can travel the distance necessary to reach your destiny. Just think: would you settle for a "quickie" love affair with a guy? Of course not! You desire a lasting love with someone who will be there for you and commit to lasting love, so why should we opt for a "quickie" love affair with the Lord of hosts, the Lover of our soul?

Tender Love from a Big God

Lasting love takes time, and God is worthy of the effort necessary. He is worthy of the spiritual cost of the journey. He wants to make this an enjoyable adventure for you and a transforming passage that you will both treasure. This experience has been provided for you by your big God. In Psalms 16:11 (KJV), the Lord provides insight into what awaits us in His presence: "Thou wilt shew me the path of life; in thy presence is fulness of joy; at thy right hand there are pleasures for evermore."

When we seek the Lord and get into His presence, the path of life is revealed to us. Things become settled within us and we begin to experience a joy like we have never known. We feel His closeness to us and new delights begin to spring up. This experience will become your own private encounter with the King of heaven and earth. In that special place, He will give you something priceless that only you alone can receive.

In Acts 2:25 (KJV), David said, "I foresaw the Lord always before my face, for he is on my right hand, that I should not be moved." God wants to make you unstoppable. The places of revelation are found in His presence. As you experience the excitement and pleasure of His presence, an amazing transformation will occur in your life.

More Whispers of Destiny

So often, I have had God whisper destiny to me in His presence, and the whispers came when I was least expecting them. I was wrapped up in my time with Him, enjoying the pleasures at His table, enjoying our time together, and then it happened. I was not expecting it; we were simply in communion, and He whispered destiny to me. I was so full of Him, so full of the joy of the Lord. Then, you know what? He did it; He leaned in closely to me and whispered things that have changed me forever: the amazing, wonderful works of the Lord.

Those moments shared at His table are special times to me. I have written many of them down to recount them back to the Lord, and many have already come to pass. There are so many pleasurable moments with Him in the secret place that my relationship with Him has become a living affair of the heart that preserves me. The Bible says, "When you call to me, I will answer you" (Psalm 91:15, GW). I am frequently in that place, feasting with the Lord, and I enjoy being there. Afterwards, when you face the world, there is a steadfast assurance and a glow that abides within you; it never diminishes or leaves.

He's Knocking

> Behold, I stand at the door and knock; if anyone hears and listens to and heeds My voice and opens the door, I will come in to him and will eat with him, and he [will eat] with Me.
> —Revelation 3:20 (AMPC)

So, He's talking about that table again. He's saying that if you will hear His voice right now, He will come in and He will sup with you, meaning that you will eat a spiritual meal together. He even says that He will reveal things to you at that table. The very meal itself is the revelation and the joy that He provides and reveals during your time of visitation at His table.

Knowing Your Value

> Who can find a virtuous woman? for her price is far above rubies. The heart of her husband doth safely trust in her, so that he shall have no need of spoil.
> —Proverbs 31:10-11 (KJV)

Too often, when we think about this virtuous woman, we look at the man that she has and all the stuff that she possesses and we think, What a lucky woman she is. We also think that she has all this stuff because this amazing man gave it all to her. Then we think, Hmm, if I could just meet a man who will do for me what this guy did for her, I would be blessed too, and my entire life would just fall into place just like hers. However, hold your horses, and let's look a little closer at this virtuous woman. Let's look at her through a different lens and inspect her life just a little bit closer to see what we find.

> She rises while it is yet night and gets [spiritual] food for her household and assigns her maids their tasks.
> —Proverbs 31:15 (AMPC)

> Charm and grace are deceptive, and beauty is vain [because it is not lasting], but a woman who reverently and worshipfully fears the Lord, she shall be praised!
> —Proverbs 31:30 (AMPC)

This is the entire key to the virtuous woman's success. Proverbs 31:15 (AMPC) says, "She rises while it is yet night and gets [spiritual] food for her household". Spiritual food. What is this spiritual food that is so important that she sacrifices sleep to get up early to acquire it? This woman knew something. She understood the importance of her relationship with the Lover of her soul. She has made an investment in her time with the Lord. She has created an asset in being closer to God than anything else in her life, and it is that investment that has created the lifestyle that she now possesses. Later, In Proverbs 31:23, the Bible makes a special mention to let you know that her husband is highly acknowledged by the elders of the city because of this virtuous woman. It is all because she is sitting at God's table early in the mornings; her meals with the Lord are affecting her entire household. This spiritual food is all the delights and pleasures that are available to each of us if we will choose to do what she did.

Your Rewards Do Not Come from Men

This woman became virtuous long before she married her husband. She was long accustomed to rising early and making her way to the secret place to be with the Lord. She was used to receiving spiritual food from God. He fulfilled her needs first and satisfied her longings long before she married the man. Because "deep calleth to deep", it was only natural for a man that was whole to be drawn to her because she was whole. You will draw what is in you towards you.

She had spent her time wisely with the Lover of her soul. Women that are still hurting from their past are often unaware that their old wounds are toxic; those toxic hurts and wounds will draw them towards broken men that will treat them badly. The virtuous woman's man was absolutely smitten by her. Her wholeness produced a glow, and it simply drew him. She did not have to run after him; she ran to the secret place.

God also gave her wisdom, making her a mover and a shaker, too. Just check her out: this woman was on top of things. In her time with Him, God was whispering mysteries to her prior to her interacting with others. He was giving her directions ahead of the need. She knew what to do before she started her day. She had insight before things happened. God showed her things to come and told her what to do. Because she was so in-tune with the Lord, she became well praised and respected. Also, let's not forget the fact that she knew how to pray and was able to block any works of darkness that would try to come against her household. It was because of her diligence that it went well with her household; her husband was highly respected at the city gates because of her. You can just hear those men saying to her husband, "Man, you really came up when you married her."

This sister was ahead of the game in every area of her life just because she had intimacy with the Lord and visited His table before she visited her own. An affair of the heart between herself and the Lord had paid off for her. Their interaction took place daily, and her life was better off because of it. She was blessed, and she knew why. Her thorough understanding and acknowledgment of what they shared together is what made the difference for her, and it shows, because God kept right on blessing her.

That is the reason her price was above rubies. You cannot blame a man for breaking his back to get to this woman. This type of woman would be in such demand from a man's perspective that if her husband that married her had not gotten to her and scooped her up, another man who loved God would have. Also, it wasn't her looks that impressed the man, either, because the Bible says in the same chapter that beauty is vain in reference to the virtuous woman, but this woman was praised because she was so filled with God.

Too often, we want the lifestyle this woman had first before seeking the Lord, but it was in seeking God that she acquired her possessions. Get before God, let Him heal your life, and the lifestyle will come. Because God found pleasure in the virtuous woman, He stamped her with His glow.

Stay Connected

God wants to connect you to the mysteries that He has for you; he wants to secure you and fasten you to Himself. Let Him make you His dovetail and become your sustaining source so that you will not be so needy that you will accept just anything that comes your way.

As I mentioned before, so many women of God have become shipwrecked because of bad choices and desperation, accepting things that add trouble to their lives. A woman of God that purposefully falls in love with Jesus, the Lover of her soul, will lose the taste for what the world has to offer after spending time at the Lord's table. So, embrace His Word.

> Sanctify them through thy truth: thy word is truth.
> —John 17:17 (KJV)

Although the Song of Solomon was written and placed in the Word of God for all believers of Christ, I believe that it was written and tailored uniquely to meet certain needs of single women of God in waiting and for women of God that are in marriages that are loveless, abusive, and deficient. God did not forget about you, woman of God. He knew you would need Him. So, He saw ahead and provided for you.

God wants you to experience a one-on-one love relationship with your awaiting Lover: Jesus Himself. This is a relationship that will satisfy the spirit and the soul. For women who are in loveless marriages and are believing God, this divine love affair with Jesus can even provoke a wayward spouse to return back to love. This love affair will make you feel beautiful inside and out as He pours the mysteries within the Song of Solomon into your heart and uses them as healing balm in your life.

The power that God will release in you will untie what binds you and heal your emotions, so you can stop making mistakes, picking the wrong men, and entering bad relationships. God will teach you what real love is and show you how real love feels. How would you like to feel what it is like to be in love long before you meet the right guy? God wants to fill your love-tank now so that when you meet someone, you will know what love is and what it is not. You will be able to protect your heart and not give in to the devil's lies, but you must have courage. You must be willing to let go of the past and you must dare to run after Him in reckless abandon. If you do, and if you are willing, He will, without fail, meet you in the secret place of the stairs.

PART 2: THE GOSPEL OF PEACE

> And your feet shod with the preparation of the gospel of peace;
>
> —Ephesians 6:15 (KJV)

Who are you, woman of God? What is your reality? Where are you going, woman of God, and why are you here? But most importantly, woman of God, what is to become of you? This is the response a woman of God gave to similar questions in Song of Solomon:

> Look not upon me, because I am black, because the sun hath looked upon me: my mother's children were angry with me; they made me the keeper of the vineyards; but mine own vineyard have I not kept.
>
> —Song of Solomon 1:6 (KJV)

Ladies, this woman made excuses. Now, even though everybody's life has hard places and even though life for her had been hard, there comes a time when excuses are no longer enough. We must face the truth, and the truth is that we are where we are because of choices, but change begins when perceptions are broken, and sometimes we have to do what we don't want to do in order to receive the things we want. However, sadly, so many of us want to be in love, but few of us know that "being in love" is waiting on us. Wrong thoughts lead to wrong feelings, and wrong feelings lead to wrong behavior.

I remember driving down the road years ago at the end of an emotionally bankrupt relationship. I was completely distraught. From deep within my heart, six little words made their way from my belly to my throat, from my throat to my mouth, and finally past my lips. I heard myself say, "I just want to feel good!" I thought, Where did that come from? However, it was true; it was genuinely how I felt. I was at the end of my rope; I was tired of feeling bad and my spirit had gotten ahead of me, speaking out loud what was really in my heart. When those desperate words came pouring out, I felt a spiritual force back away from me. Those six little words were packed with power: the power of God. God used those six little words to break the power of the devil off me. He used that situation to teach me the importance of going towards the things that make you feel good and away from the things that make you feel bad. Unfortunately, too often, we are doing the opposite; we are going toward all the things that make us feel bad, and when we get there, we feel even worse.

Healing Your Senses

When women are emotionally or physically abused, often their spiritual senses are damaged, and it becomes hard for them to hear God clearly. That is why I tell women (when they are continually making bad choices) to go towards what makes them feel good and away from what makes them feel bad. If every time you leave that person, you are left with bad feelings, you should not be with or around them. You should not be going there. So, stop going there. Move away from what makes you feel bad—the thing that is hurting you—and move toward the things that make you feel good, because God is good and He has good plans for your life.

> For I know the thoughts and plans that I have for you, says the Lord, thoughts and plans for welfare and peace, and not for evil, to give you hope in your final outcome.
> —Jeremiah 29:11 (KJV)

God wants you to know He has plans to prosper you and not harm you. He plans to give you hope and a future.

> Then you will call upon Me, and you will come and pray to Me, and I will hear and heed you. Then you will seek Me, inquire for and require Me [as a vital necessity] and find Me; when you search for Me with all your heart, I will be found by you, says the Lord, and I will release you from captivity and gather you from all nations and all the places to which I have driven you, says the Lord, and I will bring you again to the place from which I caused you to be carried away captive.
> —Jeremiah 29:12-14 (AMPC)

The Lord is making you a promise if you will seek after Him. He promises to be found by you and even bring you out of whatever has you captive and held in bondage. So many of us are in captivity right now and are feeling bad about where we are, but God is telling you to move toward the things that make you feel good and away from the things that keep making you feel so bad.

Now, listen up: I do not care if there is a circumstance that keeps hindering you. I do not care if you are on a job and you are always dreading your job and feeling bad about it; you need to find another job. God wants you to move towards the things that make you feel good and away from what makes you feel bad because God is good. So, examine the situations in your life. When you get away from that thing that continually frustrates and bothers you, stop and think about it. What is it about this situation that frustrates you? What about this makes you feel bad, and what would make you feel the goodness of God? Then, move in that direction, away from stress.

Go back in your mind over areas in your life where you are always feeling bad. What makes you feel bad all the time? You need to deal with those issues in your life, because when you're feeling good in major areas of your life, as you move forward, the blessings of God will flow. However, if you are feeling bad continuously when you are in certain situations, it may eventually affect your health. God wants you to change that. So, we must examine where we are and how and what we are feeling. We should not only cast down imaginations, but we should remove ourselves from problematic situations. God wants us to learn to meditate on His Word and think good thoughts centered around His Word.

Focus on Him

He is revealing Himself. God wants single women to focus in on Him so that He can become a husband to you, not the world. You do not have to prove a thing; He has already proved everything. He just needs your presence.

> There is difference also between a wife and a virgin. The unmarried woman careth for the things of the Lord, that she may be holy both in body and in spirit; but she that is married careth for the things of the world, how she may please her husband.
> —1 Cor. 7:34 (KJV)

God can become better and more real to you than a natural man in the flesh. He will walk with you, talk with you, and share

His secrets with you if you will lean into Him. When the time is right, He will bring the right person into your life. He wants your heart first so that you are never afraid with any amazement. God wants to teach you how to care for the things of the Lord in body and spirit. It is not about how you dress; it is about your connection to Him, knowing Him, and knowing that when He moves, you move with Him, just like that.

Real Change Must Come

God wants to change something in your life right now. You are reading this book because you can feel God tugging at your heart, He is desiring to bring real change to your door. He is aware of your need for transformation. God has a life for you that is spiritually and perfectly tailored to fit your inner being and cause your unique spiritual giftings to pop and shine!

God's power looks good on you. He is waiting to see if you are willing to seek Him. Are you willing to seek for that revelation that will transform you? He wants to cause you to come alive with His presence. Time with Him will compensate for the not-so-flattering spiritual bumps and bulges that have not been worked out yet in our lives. He will make us attractive in His presence.

Salvation is free, but growth in God has a cost. We should choose to be tailor-made by the Holy Spirit, not bargain-basement and sold cheap by the world. However, many of us are trying to get the blessing in our lives the wrong way. We want things the world's way. We want all the blessings first, and then we say we will seek God, but it does not work that way. When a person feels that they have everything they want, they do not feel the need to seek after God. You will lose your hunger for God by getting things too quickly and without developing a relationship with Him. You will become spiritually sleepy and dull of hearing. God wants you to be spiritually rich and overflowing with His presence before you gain so much that you become weary of spiritual instruction, leaving you as prey to the enemy. The God of mysteries desires to speak destinies to your heart.

Producing Good Fruit

God's mysteries carry the fruit that He desires to manifest into your life, but how are you going to get this fruit to grow in your life? Many of us have no earthly idea how to make our "God fruit" grow. We are spiritually clueless. God has a plan, and He knows how to make your life produce your purposed fruit. He knows how to make you fruitful, regardless to what you have been through. He also knows he wants to bring your desires to pass while working the plan He created for you. He wants to make your life a beautiful garden, glorious to look at. In the secret place is where it all happens. Your fruit is germinated, sprouted and produced there before God.

In His presence, I have learned the secret and I am teaching it to you: the secret is to get into the secret place. The Bible says that the woman is supposed to stay covered. Your covering is Him; He is your protection, and only God can cloak and protect you from the harsh winters of life. When a woman of God acknowledges her need to be covered by Him, she is making her first step towards the Lover of her soul. God, in His wonder and His infinite wisdom, designed the Scripture and packed it full of all the things our longing hearts need to shelter us. Those things are placed within the very words of God, just waiting to fill us.

Sweeter than the Honey in the Honeycomb

> The fear of the Lord is clean, enduring for ever; the judgments of the Lord are true and righteous altogether.

> More to be desired are they than gold, yea, than much fine gold; sweeter also than honey and the honeycomb.
> —Psalm 19:9-10 (KJV)

Precious promises and delights are housed within in the Word of God. His words are bursting with just the right ingredients, ready to feed and fill us, but we must choose to sit down and dine with Him. Taste and see that the Lord is good, check out His record: He has been faithful through the ages. Let Him fill and sustain you until the promise of God comes for you.

Ready and Prepared

Wouldn't you like to be ready and prepared? Wouldn't you prefer to be ushered into the blessing instead of being shut out from it? You are special to God and He has made provisions just for you. The table is set. Did you hear me? The God of heaven has set the table Himself for you.

Make Up Your Mind

All things are ready. I believe that if more women of God would get into the secret place, we would see more weddings in the body of Christ. More women of God would be getting married all the time, because as women become virtuous before the Lord, their lives become draped in scarlet. They become yielded to God's ways instead of their own ways, and His banner of love will wave over them, fiercely producing results.

We do not just stumble into the blessing of the Lord and into right and godly relationships. We must be emotionally and spiritually prepared to get the blessing. We must first choose to heal our lives of toxicity so that after receiving from the Lord, we are able to hold on to what He has given. You cannot play it safe to get healed, and you cannot worry about what people think and get set free. However, if you will use your faith, enter the secret place, and follow the thirty-day challenge, you will experience emotional healing, wholeness, and a one-on-one intimate relationship with the Lover of your soul.

Is Your "Believer-Meter" Working?

God is breaking open deeper revelation in the body of Christ for single, divorced, and widowed women of God. So, check your "believer-meter". Check to make sure it is working. Stop feeling bad about your past and heal it. God wants you free of your past; free of abuse, free of neglect, free of shame, and free of anything and everything that has held you back. God wants you feeling good and filled with joy. Remember, go towards what makes you feel good, because God is good, and the outcome is good, too.

God Has Not Overlooked Your Singleness

God is requesting your attendance at His table and He simply wants to know: are you ready to get your "glow" on? Are you ready to experience His divine love in a way you never have before?

The Path Of Life: Psalm 16:11

> Thou will show me the path of life: in thy presence is fulness of joy; at thy right hand there are pleasures forever more.
>
> —Psalm 16:11 (KJV)

At God's right hand, He has pleasures forevermore for you. God already has what you desire, so why go elsewhere to look for it? The pleasures you desire are at His right hand. Just meditate on that for a moment: this is where you belong. I know you may be thinking, Huh? Where do I belong, sister Toni? You belong at God's right hand. Yes, there is a place there, waiting just for you. He did not forget about your singleness. He did not forget about your need during this time. He has made special provisions just for you. So, your cry, as David's was, should be: "Lord, show me the path of life that You have for me."

You should be seeking the Lord daily to remain in His presence, because in His presence are the joys and emotional provisions that you need. Allow His presence to run over your heart like a mighty stream. Pour His glory all over your life. Allow Him to teach you about His pleasures there at His right hand. When you tell the Lord that you want Him to teach you of His pleasures, letting Him know of your desire to dine at His table, He is moved by your desire and He begins to lean in to teach you. He begins to draw close to open those pleasures up to you, to make them more accessible to you.

Allow faith to begin to rise inside your heart right now so that as you are in your own secret place with the Lord, you'll be able to clearly hear the whispers of God. I remember the first time God whispered to me; I thought someone had entered the room. God began ministering to my heart the plans He had for me. His gentle words spoke so softly to my heart and brought an eternal peace to my mind. Remember, whatever God reveals to you in the secret place belongs to you and those whispers will always line up with His Word.

> The secret things belong to the Lord our God: but those things which are revealed belong unto us and to

our children for ever, that we may do all the words of this law.

—Deuteronomy 29:29 (KJV)

Filling the Void and Taking Away the Pain

God understands our frustrations. He is really the only one who can take away our pain. Let Him fill the void and release His emotionally healing power to you. God's words are carriers of His glory and of His presence. When you meditate the Word of God, God can get the glory from His Word into you, into manifestation, and flowing throughout your life. The Bible calls it in Colossians 1:27, "Christ in you, the hope of glory", or, "Christ in you, the hope of realizing the glory".

His glory lives inside you and He wants it to manifest outside for all to see. Glory shines: it is beautiful to look upon. We crack open the shell of His glory in His presence and in His Word. We begin to mature as we abide there in that place with Him as we come to know and learn the ways of God. He becomes more precious than the most exquisite diamond. He is our reward, and as we come to know Him, we begin to realize the many wonders of His person. We begin to understand "Christ in you, the hope of glory". It is important to understand that you are betrothed to Him. His glory is a constant reminder that you definitely belong to Him.

I will not leave you comfortless: I will come to you.

—John 14:18 (KJV)

I remember the first time I heard the Lord speak the above verse to my heart. I was in the secret place in my alone time with Him. He brought me to that scripture, and as I was reading it, it leaped out at me, and I knew immediately that He was speaking directly to me. He said, "I will not leave you comfortless, I will come to you. I will come to you."

Just what do you do with that? Your Lord is softly saying those words to you right now. How do you interpret what He is saying to your heart? Do you become super spiritual and miss His meaning, or do you get all philosophical and try to conjure up a pseudo-spiritual meaning behind His gentle words? Or, in the simplicity of the Gospel, in the simplicity of who Jesus is, do you interpret that verse to exactly what He means? Do you take Him literally at His word? His words are, "I will not leave you comfortless, I will come to you." Just what do you think your Lord means by expressing that to you? What do you think Jesus is trying to convey? Are you ready to allow Him into the deepest part of your heart? Are you ready to allow him to visit you?

He is knocking at your door. In Matthew 11:28-30 (KJV), He says, "Come unto me, all ye that labour and are heavy laden, and I will give you rest. Take my yoke upon you and learn of me; for I am meek and lowly in heart; and ye shall find rest unto your souls, For my yoke is easy, and my burden is light."

PART 3: WOMEN ON FIRE

> Who maketh his angels spirits; his ministers a flaming fire;
>
> —Psalm 104:4 (KJV)

What do you suppose this verse means? Well, simply put, it means that when you get close to fire, you catch fire, or you catch on fire (we will get back to that later). When women of God are not properly connected to God, they feel unprotected, and there are so many emotions we experience even though we never tell anyone else. See if you can identify some of your thoughts and emotions below:

- Why is it that somebody else always get the blessing instead of me? I guess the blessing is not for me. I have been praying for so long, but I still have not received it.
- I will just be glad when this is all over.
- I guess I will never be happy like everybody else. I hope no one sees just how unhappy I am.
- What if something happens, what will I do?
- Always a bridesmaid, never a bride.
- Another day and nothing ever seems to change for me. I guess I will just try to keep holding on until Jesus comes back, but how much more of this can I take?

- I will just dive into my work and ignore my feelings; that will get me by.
- That man I am with does not understand me and does not even care. I am here, but just barely. I guess this relationship I am in is better than none.
- I feel so alone. I feel so left out.
- One step forward, two steps backward.
- Can't anyone see that I am hurting?
- I know he is hurting me, but if I left him, what would people think? What will the church think?
- Another bad relationship. I am so tired of this. God, help me.

These are just some of the things we tell and ask ourselves. The list goes on and on. There are many things we tell ourselves as women to get us by but let me ask you a question. Have you hurt long enough yet? Are you ready for change? If you remain attached to a false identity, you will not be prepared for the blessing. If you do not run after God, you will wind up dry, barren, fearful, bitter, desperate, and lonely.

God wants to become your spiritual blanket; the winters of life are cold without Him. He does not want you left out in the cold. Yet, many times, there are so many things we allow to hinder us. The worldly pull draws us, and without realizing it, we become too busy. We must remove interferences so that we can let God fatten us with His presence and prepare us for the winters of life.

Fire Shut Up In My Bones!

> And behold, a woman, which was diseased with an issue of blood twelve years, came behind him, and touched the hem of his garment: For she said within herself, If I may but touch his garment, I shall be whole. But Jesus turned him about, and when he saw her, he said, Daughter, be of good comfort; thy faith hath made thee whole. And the woman was made whole from that hour.
> —Matthew 9:20-22 (KJV)

Simply amazing. The reason I like this story so much is because every woman has an issue, whether she is willing to admit it or not. However, the key to success is to find the solution to our issue.

So, check out this woman. This woman is different: she was on fire with massive determination. No man could stop her, and God did not want to. Jesus acknowledged her and said, "Daughter, be of good comfort; thy faith hath made thee whole" (Matthew 9:22, KJV). Although His words proclaimed her actions and were a significant part of her healing, her own faith ignited her movement to Jesus, allowing her to quickly and quietly do just as she had purposed to do without being interrupted. This woman did not want to be identified or even recognized. She had already received a revelation from God long before she got to where Jesus was. She understood more about who He was than even the disciples. The declaration she had already made in her heart had activated a supernatural, unstoppable faith that only needed her to do that which she had decreed within herself earlier, which was to merely touch the hem of His garment. She knew if she did that, her healing would be a done deal. She had also unquestionably decided that after touching Him, she would go on about her way without bringing attention to her actions.

Although Jesus acknowledged her to seal her healing, he let her do it just as she had determined because He knew that was just how powerfully the force of her faith was operating. He was amazed by her. She possessed a boldness and understanding that put pressure on God's power to ignite the promise. This woman was on fire and took the kingdom by force; none of the people nearby even realized what had happened. Now, see her actions in the light of the scripture below:

> And from the days of John the Baptist until the present time the kingdom of heaven has endured violent assault, and violent men seize it by force [as a precious prize] a share in the heavenly kingdom is sought for with most ardent zeal and intense exertion.
> —Matthew 11:12 (AMPC)

This woman's intense exertion pulled the kingdom of God right out of the spiritual realm and into natural manifestation by force. She took a share from her heavenly bank account and withdrew from it right before their very eyes, and only Jesus knew what she had done. She did it with a smoothness that was both graceful and elegant. This woman was walking in power. This woman was on fire.

The "Martha Syndrome"

I know there was a time when it seemed that everything was simple, fresh, and good, and trusting God was easy, but now, time has passed, and a lot of things have happened. However, God wants to take you back to the time when trusting and believing Him was easy to do. He wants to remove the stinger of your past and cause your hurting heart to forget its pain so that you can serve Him like you did before.

Sometimes, we are unaware that we are neglecting God. I remember one time, when I was serving in the kingdom of God, I was doing everything that I thought would please God and others. I was much too busy, and I had neglected the things that I needed to be doing in my personal relationship with Him. I had forgotten my first Love, and my life began to suffer.

Often, we can become too busy for God or even too lazy to follow Him and seek Him. Do you know what happens as a result? A negative belief system begins to set in. We become unbelieving and ungrateful. We end up in a place where we desperately need to get before God. To get back to Him, we must first repent, then deal with the stumbling blocks we have allowed to get in the way. God does not want anything in the way of Him getting to you, and when you allow something else to come in the middle of your walk with God, it becomes an idol before Him and must be removed.

> But Martha was cumbered about much serving, and came to him, and said, Lord, dost thou not care that my sister hath left me to serve alone? Bid her therefore that she help me. And Jesus answered and said unto her, Martha, Martha, thou art careful and troubled about many things; But one thing is needful: and Mary hath chosen that good part, which shall not be taken away from her.
>
> —Luke 10:40-41 (KJV)

Martha did not realize it, but Mary was serving, just in a different way. She was busy sitting at the feet of Jesus, listening to His words, and letting them soak deep within her spirit. She did not want to miss one precious morsel of what He had to say.

The work we do in our time with the Lord is to position ourselves to receive as He pours Himself, because when Jesus is near, it is time to be still and listen. Your attitude should be worship; your posture should be praise. Many times, you will not know what He has poured into you until something occurs; you are then made aware by His Spirit that within you is the solution, and then you are able to pour.

You see, Mary was storing up all the treasures: the precious oils, the spiritual gifts, and the divine fire power that would preserve her and meet her needs and others' needs in times of trouble. Jesus said that because she has chosen this good thing to do, it will not be taken away from her and substituted with busyness and worry. Your busyness can also become an idol, even if your busyness is doing something that is theoretically good. It could be taking you away from your time with Him, especially when you know that He is tugging at your heartstrings to lean in.

You see, just because a thing is good does not mean that thing is what you should be doing. Sometimes, we are just busy for busyness's sake. Sometimes, we are busy to please the people at church, our pastor, and others, or we want to keep up appearances at work or even around the folk we think are looking at and measuring us. Sometimes, we are busy because the kids are pulling on us, but we are still neglecting our spiritual garden and running ourselves ragged for nothing. Those things and people have become idols, and whether we know it or not, we are worshipping them. They do not know your needs, nor can they meet them. So, whether your idol is a person, a place, or a thing, God wants it out of the way so that you can focus and seek Him first.

Often, after seeking the Lord, we can discern clearly what to add back into our lives and what to let go of. God does not like idols because they separate us from Him. He wants us to be committed first to Him; He knows that if we will first run after Him, He will open His hand to us and supply everything we need. He will withhold nothing and make us better mothers. God has not forgotten; He knows the things that you have need of. He is not saying, "I do not want you to have the things that you need, the things that you desire, or the things that you want." He is saying that there is a way in which He wants to order them in your life, because while the devil has a plan for you, God also has a plan. God wants us to run after the plan He has for us. When you get what you need from God, everything else will flow from that place of power.

> Now ye are clean through the word which I have spoken unto you. Abide in me, and I in you. As the branch cannot bear fruit of itself, except it abide in the vine; no more can ye, except ye abide in me.
> —John 15:3 (KJV)

Every word of God has cleansing power that will remove the stain of sin and unbelief, and as we meditate on those words, they go to work in our lives without our assistance. That is the work of the Holy Spirit of God. That is the reason it is so important that you study and meditate on the Word of God. It allows God the opportunity to wash you clean Himself. Did you know that God just cleaned you up in that area of your understanding from the words that you just read?

Many of us are trying to bear fruit outside of God. We are taking on a life outside of His Word, and it is wearing us out. You were never meant to carry life's load on your own. Jesus said that He is the one who will carry your load. God never planned for you to bear your own burdens. He is the one who is able to shoulder whatever troubles you. That is the reason He wants you to abide in Him. Abiding in Him literally means to lean into Him and remain attached to Him through the power of His Word.

Have you ever read a scripture, and when you read it, it just did something to you that you could not explain? Whether it soothed you, brought peace to you, or excited you and made you want to run all over the room, that was the power of His Word. When we access it on a continual basis and apply it to every area of our lives, it will transform us and make us whole. However, if you never spend time with God, if you never allow Him to form Christ in you, you will live ill-prepared and enter spiritual seasons of life improperly clad like the man who was invited to the wedding feast and showed up with the incorrect attire. I bet he wondered why it was such a big deal, but it was a big deal. It was disrespect. It is important to allow God to properly clad us in glorious attire that will gain us entrance to the many pleasures He has prepared, and His supernatural garments will also warm us on spiritually and emotionally cold winter nights.

God desires to dress us His way. When you dress somebody, you must first undress them of undesirable things, then wash and clean them. God wants us to take off the things that are not like Him and instead put on us the things that are like Him. God wants to undress you of the things that are not like him so that he can dress you in His likeness, but if you refuse to abide in Him, then there's nothing He can do to bring the change that you need. Jesus said, "I am the vine, ye are the branches" (John 15:5, KJV). You are His branches; you are not the vine. Some of us have gotten it mixed up; we think we are the vine. We are so busy trying to provide for ourselves that God is not able to complete the work we need within.

> Abide in me, and I in you. As the branch cannot bear fruit of itself, except it abide in the vine; no more can ye, except ye abide in me. I am the vine, ye are the branches: He that abideth in me, and I in him, the same bringeth forth much fruit: for without me ye can do nothing.
>
> —John 15:4-5 (KJV)

If you want to bear much fruit, then you must abide in Him. He has already made provisions for you. I would much rather get the provisions that God has for me than try to make provisions for myself. Just think: if this is something that only God can do, as He stated in His Word, then isn't it a mistake for us to try to do it ourselves? Unfortunately, many of us are trying to do God's job, but we are failing.

Whatever you have made of your life thus far is what you have accomplished. However, we do not have enough strength to create things eternal and lasting, but God does, and He can make it all brand-new, even our mistakes, with very little effort. What He makes for us will not cause us to cry afterwards. It will be made right.

Master Builder

God is a master builder, and He creates masterpieces all the time. We are a part of the wonderful workings of God. If we will allow Him, He will make us a masterpiece in the earthly realm. If we reject His invitation, we live within a false image of who we think we are that is based on worldly views and not based in what God says about us. I would much rather have God's image instilled in me than the image of the world. The world's image is hopeless.

The Song of Solomon is one of the key books in the Bible that we will use as God heals and restores your life. In it, there is something unique that God wants you to learn about yourself. The Song of Solomon will console you, restore you emotionally, and even lead you to love. It is a resource that God is using for single women of God in the body of Christ. God is revealing Himself within the pages to provide a source of healing, wholeness, and peace that will preserve you as you walk through dysfunction to victory. Often, we have overlooked this book, but the Holy Spirit is shedding such a light on it now because of our need.

> I am black but comely, O ye daughters of Jerusalem, as the tents of Kedar, as the curtains of Solomon. Look not upon me, because I am black, because the sun hath looked upon me: my mother's children were angry with me; they made me the keeper of the vineyards; but mine own vineyard have I not kept.
> —Song of Solomon 1:5-6 (KJV)

The first sentence of the above scripture in the Amplified Bible, Classic Edition version reads, "I am so black; but [you are] lovely and pleasant [the ladies assured her]." This woman had a complex about how she looked and felt about herself. She thought, I am too dark, my situation is so bad, nobody is going to pay any attention to me. No one will want me. However, the maidens around her were trying to encourage her.

How many of us think we are too dark? We think that our situation is too bleak or too hopeless. Maybe you think you are not good enough, not good looking enough, not the correct race or color, too old, too young, or you simply think that you have too many strikes against you. Whatever you are thinking, listen up: none of that matters to God! He is madly in love with you and wants you just the way you are.

When we think negatively about ourselves, we allow the enemy to deceive and rob us. However, changing our thinking process is easier said than done. Man looks on the outward appearance, but your Lord looks at you from your heart: the person you truly are and who He truly created you to be. The person God made you to be is forever beautiful, forever gorgeous, and forever wonderful. You are forever accepted in the Beloved. You have been specifically created the way you are for His glory, so stop neglecting your own spiritual garden.

Pit or Palace?

> I waited patiently for the Lord; and he inclined unto me, and heard my cry. He brought me up also out of an horrible pit, out of the miry clay, and set my feet upon a rock, and established my goings. And he hath put a new song in my mouth, even praise unto our God: many shall see it, and fear, and shall trust in the Lord.
> —Psalm 40:1-3 (KJV)

David is speaking, reciting the goodness of the Lord. Have you ever felt like you were in a horrible pit and God delivered you? That is how David felt. He knew God as his constant deliverer and he learned how to lean into him that way, and because God is of no respect of persons, in the same way He delivered David, He will deliver you if you will do what David did. He also wants to change you so that you never enter that pit again.

The tools God gave to David took him from tending sheep to ruling a palace and they kept Him there too. If you are in a pit and you want to get to the place God has ordained for you, you need to take heed to David's words in Psalm 40:2 (KJV): "He delivered me out of the horrible pit, out of the miry clay, and set my feet upon a rock and established my goings." That is direction; that is understanding a mystery. God spoke a mystery to David; it was about his own destiny spoken into his heart by God in the secret place. God gave him direction and established his goings. Then, He made him king and brought to pass what He had promised Him in the secret place.

God wants to give you direction and establish your goings. He wants to put a new song in your mouth like He did with David, because God is tired of you singing that same old sad song day in and day out, and you should be tired of it, too. He is saying to you, "I want to put a new song in your mouth. I want to give you new words to say." He wants genuine gladness rising within you and spontaneous praise flowing out your mouth because of what He has done and completed in you.

Psalm 40:3 (KJV) says, "Many shall see it, and fear, and shall trust in the Lord." In other words, God wants to make you a spectacle, a sign, and a wonder. Women will say, "I want what she's got! I want to be connected to her." They will be drawn to you and you will become a witness for Christ to tell them what the Lord has done in your life. The Bible says in Psalm 40:4 (KJV), "Blessed is that man that makes the Lord his trust." That person is not trusting in themselves or in things. They are not trusting in the world's ways. They are not looking at the TV to find an image to model themselves after. Rather, they are eyeing God, and the Lord is their trust. They are trusting in Him to paint the right image inside them.

> The spirit of man is the candle of the Lord, searching all the innermost parts of the belly.
> —Proverbs 20:27 (KJV)

There is a candle inside you. We are the candle of the Lord; we are the city set upon a hill so that others can see their way to God. However, for many believers, their wicks are wet, and they fail to produce light to the world. The flame they need to remain hot for God has been reduced to a mere flicker; they are just barely holding on, yet God has so much better for His daughters, and He's asking you a question:

> Behold, I am the Lord, the God of all flesh: is there anything too hard for me?
> —Jeremiah 32:27 (KJV)

Do you believe in God, or do you believe in your lying situation that is subject to change to His breath? When God speaks a word to you, it will come to pass. So, everything that the enemy has been telling you in your mind in your thoughts (because that is the battleground, where the war is fought), none of those things are true. If you are thinking thoughts such as, You are never going to have a godly relationship, or, It's just too late for you, those words are all lies, and you need to verbally cast them down. You fight the devil with the verbally spoken Word of God. No, these are not the words of God that you think to yourself in your mind, but the words of God that you dare to say out loud to Him.

Do not let the devil deceive you into not speaking. Shout the Word of God out loud so that it can work for you. Stop putting your ladder up against the wrong house by listening to the wrong words and the wrong voice. Give your attention to God and to His Word. God said in Psalm 40:6 (KJV), "Sacrifice and offering thou didst not desire; mine ears hast thou opened: burnt offering and sin offering hast thou not required." God wants your ears. He wants to recreate the way your mind thinks about you. He wants you to think the thoughts of God concerning you. Your words to God should bellow from a heart filled with praise and faith in His Word.

Prodigal Daughters

We know about the prodigal son, but there are also many prodigal daughters in the kingdom of God as well: daughters of the Lord who go out into the world to seek their destiny. Just like the prodigal son, they end up in the hog pen of life.

The parable Jesus tells in Luke 15:11-24 (KJV) is the story about a man that has two sons. The younger of the two sons told his father to give him the portion of goods that fell to him. He was rebellious, and he wanted his inheritance before the father died. He wanted it right then, so his father divided to him the portion promised to him. Many days afterward, the younger son gathered everything he had and took his journey into a far country, but in that land, he wasted away his substance with wild and rowdy living.

Lessons in the Pig Pen

Many of our choices have caused a lot of things to happen in our lives. We have made choices that were not of God because we were afraid to trust Him, so we decided to handle things ourselves for ourselves because God's way seemed too slow or seemed to not be working at all. We thought, If God is going to do it, it looks like He's taking forever. Maybe I need to get involved; maybe I need to help God out a little bit. We began going down paths we should not, thinking within, After all, I am a strong woman of God, I know what I can and cannot do. However, we fail to understand God's full intent: that the work the Lord does on the way to the blessing is often more important than the blessing itself and is necessary to produce an eternal work of glory within us that makes us impervious to the enemy. In our short-sightedness, we forfeit the gold production that is being worked in our hearts; a production that only time can produce.

It was not until the prodigal son had spent everything that he began to be in want. He got to the end of himself, found himself in a hog pen, penniless and in the middle of a famine. Only then did he remember how good things were in his father's house. Many times, we must get to the end of ourselves, to the end of our tricks, to the end of our trying before we will seek the Lord and His ways. Too often, the devil tells women, "Your time-clock is ticking. If you pass up this guy, what if nothing better comes along? You'd better take what you can get! After all, you don't want to be alone." Believe me, that thought did not come from God, it came from the devil, and you do not want one of his sons as a life partner. When you are trying to do things on your own, you are placing yourself right smack dab in the middle of the famine where there is no protection. So, if that is where you are right now, turn that desperation towards God. Become desperate enough to turn and seek the Lord.

Unfortunately, even after multiple setbacks, many women will continue seeking "Mr. Right", even though God has just delivered them. They try repeatedly to make love happen for themselves because the feelings of loneliness and desperation seem overwhelming. It becomes a vicious cycle and can even pass down to their own daughters if they do not break it. Stop holding onto relationships that you know are ungodly and harming you and your children. You are feeding swine. Stop it, because a pig is a pig, no matter how you dress it up. Wipe your crying eyes and get on your face before God. I did, and you can do it, too. He will heal you, make you whole, then give you what you need. When God's daughters come to themselves, He makes them complete and impenetrable to the enemy.

Coming to Ourselves

I remember a situation with my oldest daughter when she was just a little girl. She was going through the out-of-control "terrible twos" that young mothers dread. However, I was really the one going through the "terrible twos", because she was running all over the place getting into things and I was the one constantly chasing after her, trying to catch her before she got into too much trouble.

Church had become the hotspot where she seemed to really get busy and loose, so I had to keep a switch handy during Sunday services. I would pray every Sunday, Lord, please do not let her run around the church today. However, every time, like clockwork, right after worship service, she would jump off the children's bench and run around the church, so I would have to run after her with my switch to try to catch her before she got too far out of hand. I would take her to the bathroom to talk to her, sometimes spank her, quiet her down, then bring her back into service. This went on for weeks, and frankly, I had begun to dread going to service, but I went in faith anyway every Sunday, and every time we'd get to church, she would run around all over again.

However, one Sunday, everything changed all at once. As usual, she was sitting with the other kids at the end of the same row that I was sitting on, and, as normal, the worship service was ending, which was ordinarily her que to get up and run, so I had begun balancing myself, preparing to run after her. I leaned forward and looked down the bench towards her, pointing the switch in her direction, ready to make my gracious dash. She steadied herself as well to stand up just as the song was ending, but for some strange reason, this time, she glanced down the row towards me. She stared for a good minute at the switch I was holding in my hand, directed and slanted towards her, as if she was debating and gauging within herself what to do, and for the first time in weeks, she changed her mind. She leaned back on the bench and sat back down. Oddly enough, she remained seated until the end of the service. I was amazed.

After that time, she never ran in church again. My daughter saw that switch that had chastised her for weeks and finally came to herself. Her transformation took place that day. She became wiser, and I rested. Sometimes, the chastening we are experiencing is meant to cause us to come to ourselves and sit back down to hear God.

Coming Home

After demanding his inheritance from his father, the prodigal son left home with his nose high in the air. However, he soon returned, humbled by his painful hog pen experience. He returned emotionally and physically drained, shamed, and without resistance. With his head bowed, he assumed a posture of compliance and said to his father, as documented in Luke 15:18-19 (KJV), "Father, I have sinned against heaven, and before thee, And am no more worthy to be called thy son: make me as one of thy hired servants."

The prodigal son had been transformed. He understood now that his father was wise and loving. He realized his father had done everything to protect Him from the cruelties of the world. He also realized that he had been short sighted and that he did not know what to do with his life, but his father knew his purpose. He needed a connection to his father. He needed his father's compassion, wisdom, and direction. He needed to be made by him, just as we each need to be made by God. God has a plan for us, and that plan is incredibly good.

There is a fresh wind of the Spirit blowing in your direction. Wisdom is crying in the streets to God's daughters: "Seek the Lord." Stop the madness you are drowning in. You need His presence just so you can sleep at night. Your heart is longing for Him. He has created something within you that craves for Him, but your head has confused you with desires for natural men, trying to use it to fill your longings. However, you cannot survive without the King of your heart.

Never Forget Lo-Debar

Often, the worst places of our lives can become the places where God reveals His covenant plans for us. After King David took the throne of Saul, most of Saul's family had been killed; there were none left alive except a son of Jonathan named Mephibosheth, who was lame in his feet. Mephibosheth had been accidentally crippled by his nurse, who was trying to get him to safety as she fled from David's army.

> And Jonathan, Saul's son, had a son that was lame of his feet. He was five years old when the tidings came of Saul and Jonathan out of Jezreel, and his nurse took him up, and fled: and it came to pass, as she made haste to flee, that he fell, and became lame. And his name was Mephibosheth.
>
> —2 Samuel 4:4 (KJV)

Mephibosheth, now a crippled adult, was in hiding and living in fear of being discovered by David, the king. Yet, in his alone time, David remembered his covenant promise to Jonathan that he would show kindness to Jonathan's family no matter what. Moved to honor his promise to Jonathan, David had compassion for Saul's family and asked a question concerning the descendants of Saul.

> And David said, Is there yet any that is left of the house of Saul, that I may show him kindness for Jonathan's sake?
>
> —2 Samuel 9:1 (KJV)

David discovered Mephibosheth, the son of Jonathan, and told one of his servants to go and fetch him from the place where he was hiding, a place called Lo-debar. Lo-debar was a very undesirable place with many undesirable people, but unbeknownst to Mephibosheth, David was about to change his life and bring him into restoration and destiny. David fetched Mephibosheth from Lo-debar, brought him to his table, and restored all the land of Saul to him as well. Mephibosheth received a permanent place at David's table because of his father's covenant promise with the king.

David got his understanding and illustration of a covenant from God. David's understanding of a covenant was eternal: he understood that a covenant applies to everyone that is related to the person he made covenant with. Because Jonathan and David had a covenant, every relation of Jonathan mattered to David. After becoming king, David could have ignored his covenant agreement with Jonathan. After all, Jonathan was dead. However, David understood the importance of the covenant and he honored their agreement.

David did not forget his covenant with Jonathan, and God has not forgotten His covenant with you. That promise from God to you applies to your children and family as well. God is ready to do something in your Lo-debar. God is fetching you from your Lo-debar and restoring your destiny. Prophetically, God told me, "Go, fetch My daughters and bring them out of Lo-debar." God wants you out of Lo-debar. Everything you thought you had lost; God is wanting to restore. God spoke to my heart to fetch His daughters out of Lo-debar who are hurting and to bring them to His table so that they may eat and dine with Him continually.

God wants you out of Lo-debar, but some of us are trying to hold on to Lo-debar. God said to get out of Lo-debar, because nothing good is going to happen there. Lo-debar is your past; what God has for you is your future. You are the Lord's dovetail; He wants to restore you. He wants to bring His promises to pass in your life and give you your heart's desire. There is nothing to fear with Jesus beside you. At His table, there is healing for your heart, your soul, your body, and your mind.

Say out loud, "I will never forget Lo-debar," and RSVP in your heart right now by saying, "Lord, I accept the challenge to connect and fall in love with You and keep You as the King of my heart and the Lover of my soul." It is time to refocus and start receiving heaven on earth right now.

PART 4: THE COST

Spank Her Now or Cry Later

My daughters are ten years apart in age, but they are awfully close and best friends to each other. I have a special bond with each of them and I thank God for allowing me the privilege of leading them each to Christ at separate times. However, my relationship with them is distinct even to this day, because not only were their personalities so unique, but while growing up, they were a generation apart in age.

> Now no chastening for the present seemeth to be joyous, but grievous: nevertheless, afterward it yieldeth the peaceable fruit of righteousness unto them which are exercised thereby. Wherefore lift up the hands which hang down, and the feeble knees; And make straight paths for your feet, lest that which is lame be turned out of the way; but let it rather be healed. Follow peace with all men, and holiness, without which no man shall see the Lord: Looking diligently lest any man fail of the grace of God; lest any root of bitterness springing up trouble you, and thereby many be defiled;
> —Hebrews 12:11-15 (KJV)

I always kept my baby girl close to me because we both had a hard time during her birthing process. So, on the day she was born, she became my "hip-baby". In other words, from the time she arrived, I placed her on my hip, and that was that. She was a quiet and reserved child, so other kids tended to pick on her, which bothered me more than it bothered her. She seemed initially to take it all in stride, but over time, I noticed that their hurtful actions towards her caused her to act out and do things that she was directly told by me not to do. When I would begin scolding her, she would immediately promise never to do it again, so I would let her off easy and without consequences. This went on for a while, and because she was already facing opposition from other children, overlooking her disobedience in what I felt like were small areas seemed minor to me. So, I would correct her with my words only, but with no real discipline behind them because I did not want her to cry.

This continued until God began to deal with my heart in the middle of the night. He showed me the results of not disciplining her when she really needed it, and what He showed me made me cry. I understood then that although it would be painful initially to spank her, it would bring self-control and restraint into her life along with other righteous fruit that Christ would use later to guide her. I awakened her and disciplined her right then and there, and whenever I gave in in ways that I shouldn't have, the Holy Spirit would alert me that I needed to correct her. Whenever it happened, I would spank her, often with tears streaming down my face, and within a short time, we stopped having those issues. I also taught her the importance of forgiving others that hurt and wounded her in order to remove all bitterroots that tried to spring up because of what they had done.

God healed her heart and set her free. That was years ago. I also remember when my baby girl climbed down off my hip and became an amazing woman of God. Years later, I repented to her for waking her to discipline her instead of waiting until the next day, and she graciously forgave me, too. Thank you, sweetheart.

Special Note:

No, you cannot turn back the hands of time. You cannot undo what has been done. However, you have a tool that is more progressive. You have the tool of forgiveness. Your forgiveness is a weapon against the enemy that only you can wield. So, live your life so that the transgressions of others become your power to rise. The degree to which you are able to forgive is the same magnitude to which you will receive God's supernatural power force to soar.

His Taste Heals and Soothes

> Let him kiss me with the kisses of his mouth: for thy love is better than wine. Because of the savor of thy good ointments thy name is as ointment poured forth, therefore do the virgins love thee. Draw me, we will run after thee: the king hath brought me into his chambers: we will be glad and rejoice in thee, we will remember thy love more than wine: the upright love thee.
> —Song of Solomon 1:2-4 (KJV)

The women in this verse are single women. They are expressing their feelings about their Beloved. They are enjoying Him to the fullest. Every moment with Him is filled with delight and pleasure and they are carefully taking it all in so that they do not miss anything that He is providing. They do not want to leave His presence. They are head over heels in love with Him. They want Him to draw them because they recognize their need to run after Him. His aroma is spiritually intoxicating to them; even His name provides a soothing balm that they need.

Balm from Gilead

> Is there no balm in Gilead; is there no physician there? Why then is not the health of the daughter of my people recovered?
>
> —Jeremiah 8:22 (KJV)

Truly, the Lord Himself is a spiritual medicine that can heal our bodies, our spirits, and our minds. God wants the health of His daughters restored. He does not want you wounded and unrecovered. There is still medicinal ointment available for His daughters if they will run after Him to get what they need. He knows how to apply the perfect mixture to our individual hearts to heal our wounded souls.

The Word of God says in Jeremiah 8:22 (KJV), "Is there no balm in Gilead?" The Bible declares that balm is for healing and preservation. God's balm possesses a healing and keeping power; it is like an anointed lotion. His balm is soothing to your spiritual body and will safeguard you on your way to the blessing. God wants to saturate you with His balm. His balm comes from the Holy Spirit. However, we have been robbed of His presence; we have been robbed of His power, a power that is ever ready to heal and preserve us. Although we have the right to it, we have not accessed it; yet it still waits for us, on the ready to supply what we need.

It is time to step into the deeper things of God. We must become desperate for more. We must desire more of Him and we must stop leaning on the world for comfort. That is what the single women decided in the Song of Solomon. They thought, Hey, I realize You have everything I need. They came to themselves, made a declaration, and ran after Him.

Actions Bring Change

The single women's actions in the Song of Solomon profoundly changed their lives for good. When they made the decision to run after Him, their destiny was immediately reformed. He became their lodging place. He provided everything that they needed. God wants you to run after Him because He has everything you need. This is a crucial attitude that every single woman in the body of Christ must have in this delicate hour. She must desire Him more than the very breath she breathes because it does not matter who you meet, get involved with, or even who you decide to marry. No mere man can ever truly heal your heart and fill the place that is designed for Him except Him. That place is for Him and Him alone.

Knowing the purpose of God for our lives brings peace and an overall resolve to us. We can stop worrying about the future; we are no longer anxious, and things become settled for us. You will begin to live within a joy that you never thought possible, a joy you never knew existed. It is not a worldly joy; it is not an earthly joy. It is an unexplainable joy of the kingdom of God. It originates directly from the kingdom of God, released into your heart without your effort. It is one of His gifts to you for your surrender. That is just one of the delights waiting for you at His table.

Imagine the Most Beautiful Table You've Ever Seen

Often, we shut ourselves out from what may be possible through rationalization, but the things of God are activated by the spirit, not by the flesh. It is not through the natural mind that we receive salvation, but through faith in God through Jesus Christ. It was His blood sacrifice that paid the ransom for our sins, and because He took our place and died for us, we now have eternal life. His precious blood can cleanse our souls and make us whole. However, we must take the steps necessary to get to His table.

Just imagine a beautiful table that is set for two lovers. The man is there, waiting for the one he loves to arrive. He has a beautiful gift there at the table waiting for her. He waits and waits, but she never arrives. She misses their date. God has made an appointment with you, and your gift is sitting there, waiting for you. He is hoping you will show up.

The Woman with the Alabaster Box

Jesus tells the story of the woman with the alabaster box. She offers an incredibly unique situation, and you can tell in the scripture that the Lord takes great pride when he talks about this woman. Jesus does more than simply discuss her plight with Peter; He discusses her out loud because He wants her situation and predicament marked as an example, not only for everyone present that day, but also for everyone that would read about her afterwards. He did this so that they would not only understand her tenacity towards God in the face of a contemptable crowd, but they would also understand how God, not man, views this precious woman. So, read the scripture carefully:

> And, behold, a woman in the city, which was a sinner, when she knew that Jesus sat at meat in the Pharisee's house, brought an alabaster box of ointment. And stood at his feet behind him weeping, and began to wash his feet with tears, and did wipe them with the hairs of her head, and kissed his feet, and anointed them with the ointment. Now when the Pharisee which had bidden him saw it, he spake within himself, saying, This man, if he were a prophet, would have known who

and what manner of woman this is that toucheth him: for she is a sinner. And Jesus answering said unto him, Simon, I have somewhat to say unto thee. And he saith, Master, say on. There was a certain creditor which had two debtors: the one owed five hundred pence, and the other fifty. And when they had nothing to pay, he frankly forgave them both. Tell me therefore, which of them will love him most? Simon answered and said, I suppose that he, to whom he forgave most. And he said unto him, Thou hast rightly judged. And he turned to the woman, and said unto Simon, Seest thou this woman? I entered into thine house, thou gavest me no water for my feet: but she hath washed my feet with tears, and wiped them with the hairs of her head. Thou gavest me no kiss: but this woman since the time I came in hath not ceased to kiss my feet. My head with oil thou didst not anoint: but this woman hath anointed my feet with ointment. Wherefore I say unto thee, Her sins, which are many, are forgiven; for she loved much: but whom little is forgiven, the same loveth little. And he said unto her, Thy sins are forgiven.

—Luke 7: 37-48 (KJV)

This is How God Views You, Woman of God!

Despite what has happened in your life, despite what was done to you, despite what you did, God loves you and He wants to settle things in your life. All power has been delivered unto Jesus through His finished work at the cross; He desires to forgive and remove everything that has wounded, hurt, and held you back. He wants to remove the sting of those memories through the authority of His Word and the power of His shed blood.

This woman knew that Jesus was her only hope, and she had become desperate enough to not care anymore what others thought about her. She was willing to risk being exposed to be set free. So, she made her way to Jesus, and there she got exactly what she came for. Jesus made her brand-new, and no man had ever been able to give her that. Jesus recognized her tenacity to forge ahead to make her way to Him and her courage to minister to Him in the face of opposition. His love for her was so secure that as He explained her dilemma out loud to Simon, He purposefully turned and withdrew Himself from the staring eyes of the ninety-nine who were there judging her; instead, he attentively praised and spoke of her efforts directly. Then, as He slowly turned to look at the woman, while still speaking to Peter of her kindnesses towards Him, all eyes were on the two of them as a calm silence filled the room. In that moment, as she was standing before Him, it was as if it was just she and Jesus alone. Jesus praised her labor towards Him, and with compassion, He forgave and removed the weight of her sins, making her whole right in front of them all. She left that place set free, with nothing missing, nothing broken, and with nothing hanging from her any longer but the glory of God.

Removing the Veil

God wants to remove the veil from your heart. The veil is the thing that separates you from true union with Him. It keeps you from seeing clearly. I remember once, when basking in His presence, feeling His balm saturating my spirit and my soul. My natural body became like spaghetti under the weight of His glory. I literally could not stand up; His presence was so strong and the anointing so heavy. I could feel His arms as they wrapped around me, comforting me. God wants to hide you in His pavilion away from whatever storm you are facing so that He can bring you out into a better place in life after the storm passes.

Wisdom vs. Foolishness

Then shall the kingdom of heaven be likened unto ten virgins, which took their lamps, and went forth to meet the bridegroom. And five of them were wise, and five were foolish. They that were foolish took their lamps, and took no oil with them; But the wise took oil in their vessels with their lamps. While the bridegroom tarried, they all slumbered and slept. And at midnight there was a cry made, Behold, the bridegroom cometh; go ye out to meet him. Then all those virgins arose, and trimmed their lamps. And the foolish said unto the wise, give us of your oil; for our lamps are gone out. But the wise answered, saying, Not so; lest there be not enough for us and you; but go ye rather to them that sell, and buy for yourselves. And while they went to buy, the bridegroom came; and they that were ready went in with him to the marriage: and the door was shut. Afterwards came also the other virgins, saying, Lord, Lord, open to us. But he answered and said, Verily I say unto you, I know you not. Watch therefore, for ye know neither the day nor the hour wherein the Son of man cometh.

—Matthew 25:1-13 (KJV)

Choose Change

I believe that we are prophetically living in the time of the ten virgins in the above verses. This is the time to examine your life as never before. It is time to remove all stumbling blocks of sin and get things right with God. It is time to stop making the same old mistakes, taking breaks from God and falling in and out of God and godliness so you can avoid being "cooked in the squat" or caught in your sin. Remove the anger and resentment about what has happened in your life. Your future depends on what you do now.

I believe God gives us grace despite ourselves, but the devil hates you. He wants you to think you can continue doing things the same way you have always done them without consequences. He wants you to make moves that keep you from living inside the will of God. Satan's desire is that you be shut out when the bridegroom cometh.

God is trying to reach His daughters now. The Bible says to examine your life to see whether you are walking in the faith. It implies that you must examine your own life, not the preacher, not the minister, and not your sister friend. You must do your own examination. You must become naked before Him about where you stand in your life and be willing to do whatever work is necessary to get to a better place. Do not be foolish and get played by the devil by holding onto what has happened, because it is not worth what it could cost you.

Observe the Actions of the Wise Virgins

All the virgins were waiting for their "dream man". Outwardly, they all seemed pretty much the same, but the scripture makes it clear that they were not the same. In fact, five were wise and five were foolish. In other words, five were prepared and five were not. The distinct actions of each virgin speaks to her own character development. There was preliminary work that the wise virgins did that the foolish virgins omitted. So, although outwardly it appeared as though they were the same, they were not. What they each chose to do prior to the waiting period became the deciding factor to their individual fate. The wise virgins were special. Often, we see women of God burning with God's light and we wonder how it is that when they pray, things happen, their faith remains unshaken in the midst of hardship, they live within a calm assurance, and they seem to know something others do not.

The Secret of the Wise

A price had been paid by the wise virgins. It cost them a lot to make sure there was enough oil in their lamps. Although they were waiting alongside the foolish virgins, they were distinctly different. Now, the difference between them did not show up immediately, but it showed up at midnight. Midnight is usually the darkest hour of our lives. What will you do at the midnight hour of your life? Are you prepared for it? Have you stored up that which is needed to go the distance that will take you to your promise, or are you still living on spiritual oil that you know is not sufficient? God wants you freshly filled with His presence. He wants you healed and whole from the inside out so that no matter what comes your way, the wisdom of His Holy Spirit can light your pathway and lead you to victory.

It is time for the daughters of the King to stop being foolish and become wise. Stop trying to bring your plans to pass when God already has plans for you. It is time to abandon your own ways, because your ways have hurt and destroyed your life. It is time to turn back to God and allow Him to do a work within you. He will remove what needs removing and fill you with His oil of gladness. A lack of oil is a lack of preparation for your journey.

It's Hard To Build A Tent In The Rain

Do not be foolish and wait until things happen to try to begin putting oil in your lamp. When the cry came at midnight, the foolish virgins asked the wise virgins for some of their oil, but the wise answered, "Not so, lest there be not enough for us and you; but go rather to them that sell and buy for yourselves" (Matthew 25:9, KJV). The wise virgins knew the preciousness of the oil that they possessed. Their time spent in the secret place had produced their priceless oil and they correctly estimated its value. You can see how irresponsible the foolish virgins were, asking for something so precious without understanding its value. However, the wise virgins knew what it had cost them to make the purchase. Even though they realized the foolish virgins were in a desperate predicament, they still refused to let go of any of their prized oil.

The Amplified Bible also says that the wise virgins draped on and carried about themselves extra flask of oil. They were literally covered with oil containers that were filled to the brim with their costly emollient. They were taking no chances of not having enough. They had brought enough to wait however long it might take the bridegroom to arrive. Their hard work and extra time with the Lord—intimately getting to know Him and letting Him fill them with Himself—was paying off. You cannot just give that away to someone. It had cost them, and the wise virgins understood that the foolish virgins must go buy that type of purchase themselves.

I can imagine the wise virgins getting up early in the morning before the Lord, then staying up late at night before Him. Whenever they heard Him whisper, they would lean in for more, not lean away from Him and go back to bed. They gave up sleep just to know Him. They would drop everything when it came time to get before Him. They yearned for Him, learning His ways and His voice. No, you cannot just cavalierly give that away, and you cannot just explain why you will not release your oil either, as that would take too long. No, the one in need of the oil must go do what you did and acquire it for themselves.

The wise virgins were aware of what the oil had cost them, and there was no time for sharing or explaining. Their wisdom came while in the process of manufacturing and garnering their costly oil. The process had taught them much, so they were not careless about any of its significance. They were focused only on the prize, and their prudence paid off, preparing them for their coming bridegroom. When He arrived, they received what they had worked long and diligently for and joyfully went in to meet Him.

A Lampstand for God

You are God's lampstand; your life is supposed to shine brightly before Him. His oil is your preservation, it is a spiritual treasure, but you must seek it out to make your purchase. You must decide which of these women you will be. By not deciding, you are deciding by default. It does not matter how long you have been on your journey with the Lord; whether it be five, ten, twenty-five years or more, or even if you've just known the Lord for one day, you need more of Him. Extraordinarily little or no oil in your spiritual lamp will cause you to burn out at the time you need it most, and you will not know that time is coming until it arrives. So, fill up now. Prepare now. It is extremely easy to be a foolish virgin, to just do nothing in Christ, to not fill your lamp with oil, to not repent, to not seek after God, and to continue blaming others. It takes absolutely no effort to qualify as one of the foolish virgins.

Wisdom is Never Jealous

You never have to be jealous of something that someone has gotten from the Lord, because our God is a God with no respect of persons. However, sometimes individuals are receiving because of diligence, time spent, and obedience to God, and He is simply rewarding them. At times, God's plan may be heading in a different direction than what you thought and you are simply missing it, but you will never know clarity until the Lord can develop your spiritual ears enough to hear and obey Him. Your blessings are always on the path He has designed for you, but you need Him to light the way. You are responsible now for what you know. So, get busy allowing Him to teach you the path of life He has for you. You do not have to create a path, just submit yourself and allow Him to teach and direct you to yours.

Every Tub Has to Sit on Its Own Bottom

Although the wise virgins did not share their own oil with the foolish virgins, they did redirect them to the place where oil could be purchased. We must become responsible to feed ourselves in Christ, to read His Word and obey His promptings. We must grow up in Christ and intimately get to know Him for ourselves. It is good to listen to spiritual leaders, but ultimately, God wants you to know His voice for yourself.

You purchase oil with God as you spend time with Him, learning from Him in the secret place. There, He reveals Himself to you and strengthens your heart for the future. However, the saddest thing of all to me in this chapter is that the foolish virgins rush out to buy oil, only to return and be shut out of the blessing. My heart weeps for the women of God that are being shut out of the blessing. If you do not do the work, you will not be ready, you will not be prepared, and you will be shut out. As you are reading these words right now, you can repent for where you have missed God, turn from your own ways, allow God to fill your lampstand with Himself, and burn brightly for His glory.

Increase Your Oil by Spending Time with the Lord

One part of waiting in the Lord's presence is praying until the release comes. Then, soak there in worship after prayer is done. As you soak in His presence, you are soaking in the Lord Himself as He oils you and comes to your aid, answering your prayer. The Lord promises to propel us into good seasons of blessings. There is a balm in Gilead to heal our wounded souls. He knows how to soothe our inflamed hearts and quiet our emotions. His healing balm will soothe us and position us for the future He has planned for us. In your time of visitation, you can be foolish, or you can be wise; I pray you choose the latter.

PART 5: EXTRACTING GOLD

Healing Opens the Door for Real Love

Sometimes, your waiting for the promise seems long, but trust God as Joseph did and see what he does:

> He is [earnestly] mindful of His covenant and forever it is imprinted on His heart, the word which He commanded and established to a thousand generations, The covenant which He made with Abraham, and His sworn promise to Isaac, Which He confirmed to Jacob as a statute, to Israel as an everlasting covenant, Saying, Unto you will I give the land of Canaan, as your measured portion, possession and inheritance. When they were but a few men in number, in fact, very few, and were temporary residents and strangers in it, When they went from one nation to another, from one kingdom to another people, He allowed no man to do them wrong; in fact, He reproved kings for their sakes, Saying, Touch not My anointed, and do My prophets no harm. Moreover, He called for a famine upon the land [of Egypt]; He cut off every source of bread. He sent a man before them, even Joseph, who was sold as a servant. His feet they hurt with fetters; he was laid in chains of iron and his soul entered into the iron, Until his word [to his cruel brothers] came true, until the word of the Lord tried and tested him. The king sent and loosed him, even the ruler of the peoples, and

let him go free. He made Joseph lord of his house and ruler of all his substance,

—Psalm 105: 8-21 (AMPC)

I understand the verses above and how waiting for the promise sometimes seems long, because there was a time years ago when my brokenness caused me to turn and walk away from the man that I am in love with and married to today. Thankfully, he never married, until twenty-five years later, when he married me.

You see, I grew up in a very abusive home, and by the time I was eighteen, my emotions had been shattered multiple times. However, I always credit my oldest daughter for getting me saved when she was just a baby, because it was after her birth that I accepted Christ. I remember laying her in her baby carrier beside me as I sat on the floor of my empty house. I took one look at her, and my eyes filled with tears. I bowed my head, and asked Jesus Christ to save me, fill me with the Holy Spirit, and make me a good mother. He immediately saved me right there on the floor, filled me with the Holy Spirit, and made me a good mother, too.

Sadly, you can never outrun your trauma. No, the trauma of your past must be healed, or it will follow you. I started out in ministry early after becoming saved. I was busy helping so many women yet trying to survive in a toxic marriage. However, it was not until I healed my life that the bad relationships stopped, and I walked out of toxicity for good. So, I know what it is like to be single, divorced, or widowed. However, because emotional wholeness draws men that are whole to you, healing your heart and accepting God's love is all you need to do. His love will draw what you need when the time is right without fail.

After becoming saved, I always wondered through the years why I would frequently have this dream of an amazing wedding as if it were my wedding day. Each time I would have the dream,

I would awaken, pray, and wonder what the dream meant, that is, until twenty-five years later, at age fifty-seven, it all became plain when the dream became a reality and I walked down the aisle, turned to face him, and married the man in my dreams. Yes, the man I walked away from twenty-five years earlier was the same man I said yes to that day; we picked up where we had left off twenty-five years later. My wholeness simply drew him back to me.

Over time, I have watched God transform every hard place and make everything beautiful in its time. Like Joseph, I have discovered the power of laying between the words of God until the Word of the Lord comes for you. Just like the phoenix rising from the ashes, fearless, untouchable, and powerful, I, too, have seen what God can do. When you heal your life, God will make His plans your reality no matter how long it takes, because God's love never fails.

> Love bears up under anything and everything that comes, is ever ready to believe the best of every person, its hopes are fadeless under all circumstances and it endures everything [without weakening]. Love never fails—never fades out or becomes obsolete or comes to an end.
>
> —1 Corinthians 13:7-8 AMPC

Golden Nuggets

We are only mere broken jars of clay, but in His presence, He will mold us. At His table, we discover an uncommon love. We become a garden enclosed just for Him, and our desire is towards Him, our Beloved, not towards a man. Our hearts run after Him and search for banners of His love. Through this journey, the Spirit of God will be able to satisfy us and remove the ungodly desires and actions that lead us astray. God wants to reset our spiritual clocks and fill us with Himself as he did with the five wise virgins. He wants to give you the ability to go the distance, to meet your destiny, and ultimately connect with a godly love that is yet to come, if you desire one.

Clues of Understanding

What are the clues placed within the kingdom that lead us to our Beloved? Our God has left golden nuggets of understanding throughout His Word. They serve as spiritual breadcrumbs that lead us to Him. They also feed us as we travel. They are the tracks we follow; they speak solely of Him, they teach us His ways, and they communicate His heart, thoughts, and plans for us. We must believe Him, take Him at His Word, then climb to the secret place. If we doubt Him, we must be honest with Him about our fears and we must forgive so that doubts can be neutralized, stumbling blocks can be removed, and our faith can be preserved. God wants your faith preserved, because cares and fears are weights too heavy to carry. We must remove them by laying it all before Him, confessing them and then continuing our journey. We must travel light. We are only able to carry a lamp and bring extra oil for the journey.

Who Is This King?

The hearts of the world are crying out, Who is this King who desires to be the lover of my soul? Allow Him to set your heart aflame; you are ravishing to Him, and He wants to dance with you in the holy place. Where could you go that would separate you from Him? Wherever you turn, He's already there. You did not choose Him, He chose you; His gaze is with you. He will never let go; He surrenders to you in the secret place, declaring, I'm yours, you're mine, forever. God is steadfast and unmovable, even when we are not. He wants to look upon you and dress you in garments that will prepare you for your destiny.

Your encounter with the Lord during your approaching thirty-day challenge is just ahead. It will transform your life and change you forever. You will learn to enjoy Him on a different level and in a different way.

Know Him

Paul said, "That I may know him, and the power of his resurrection, and the fellowship of His sufferings, being made conformable unto His death;" (Philippians 3:10, KJV). In the Amplified Bible, Classic Edition version, the same verse reads like this:

> [For my determined purpose is] that I may know Him [that I may progressively become more deeply and intimately acquainted with Him, perceiving and recognizing and understanding the wonders of His Person more strongly and more clearly], and that I may in that same way come to know the power outflowing from His resurrection [which it exerts over believers], and that I may so share His sufferings as to be continually transformed [in spirit into His likeness even] to His death, [in the hope]
> —Philippians 3:10 (AMPC)

God wants to teach you the wonders of His person more strongly and more clearly. In the secret place of the stairs, you will learn to enjoy Him that way, because after all, you are betrothed to Him and you are going to be with Him forever. So, why not get to know Him now? His provisions are ever ready for you there.

Receive the Blessing

If you are running after the blessing, you will never catch it. God did not create you to run after blessings, things, or anyone except Him. God commanded us to seek first the kingdom of God and His righteousness. Then, He promised to add everything else we need to our account.

When women of God awaken to the call and begin seeking after Him, they become so caught up in God that finding a mate no longer matters to them. They learn how to get spiritual food for their households. They realize that He was the one their soul was longing for all along, not a man. A peace comes that they are unwilling to relinquish or walk away from. Things become settled within them, and that is when it happens. That is when the blessings and the desires of their hearts begin to show up. Suddenly, all their needs are met, and the work completed in them by God has produced a virtuous woman. When your spiritual tank is filled with His oil, you can begin to enjoy your life's journey. The scenery looks better because you are at peace. You are not worried about running out of oil, because you are filled and strapped with more than enough; daily, He is loading you with benefits, and you are ready to face whatever is up ahead because you are safely covered and hidden in Him. Yes, you are prepared to wait however long it takes to enter in, because the longer it takes, the brighter you glow.

The King

The Spirit of the Lord God is upon me; because the Lord hath anointed me to preach good tidings unto the meek; he hath sent me to bind up the brokenhearted, to proclaim liberty to the captives, and the opening of the prison to them that are bound; To proclaim the acceptable year of the Lord, and the day of vengeance of our God; to comfort all that mourn; To appoint unto them that mourn in Zion, to give unto them beauty for ashes, the oil of joy for mourning, the garment of praise for the spirit of heaviness; that they might be called trees of righteousness, the planting of the Lord, that he might be glorified. And they shall build the old wastes, they shall raise up the former desolations, and they shall repair the waste cities, the desolations of many generations.

—Isaiah 61:1-4 (KJV)

Let It Flow

Any time revelation flows from the written Word of God, it is an indication that the Holy Spirit is highlighting that scripture for a purpose. As you continue to roll the words of that scripture over and over in your mind, a deeper understanding of what the scripture means and what God is trying to directly convey to you will begin to fill your heart. That is God speaking to you by His Spirit.

In the above scripture, an announcement foretelling of Jesus and the works that He would do in the earth is being proclaimed by the prophet Isaiah. This announcement speaks of coming restoration and liberation to the people of God. It highlights the marvelous works of God toward a lost and dying mankind. Jesus, through His sacrifice on the cross, tasted death for all men so that we could enjoy salvation and the abundant life offered through His resurrection.

Although much has been done by God to bring you this amazing gift, if you do not access the outflow of His resurrection and what it provides, it is as though deliverance did not occur for you. God has redeemed and rescued you from your past; you must activate your freedom. Jesus has reclaimed your liberty. He is saying, "I am opening that prison that you have been locked away in. I am delivering you out of captivity." He came by His Spirit to bind up your broken heart, to make you whole, and to speak liberty to every part of your life. Every part of who you are and who you have been created to be, He's bringing it back into divine alignment right now and establishing it in your hearing as you read. God is positioning your life for something brand-spanking-new. He is speaking all things back into divine order in your life in His presence, in His name.

Beauty for Ashes

God said in Isaiah 61:1-4 (KJV) that He came to appoint unto them that mourn in Zion, to give them beauty for ashes, the oil of joy for mourning, the garment of praise for the spirit of heaviness that they might be called trees of righteousness, the planting of the Lord, that He might be glorified. God wants glory out of your life, and the only way He can get glory out of you is to smear Himself all over you so that you can gleam brightly with the light of His presence; He offers His beauty for your ashes. I said out loud one day, "I just want to feel good!" God healed my life and replaced my sorrow with gladness.

God wants to make you beautiful from the inside out. God will give you joy to replace all your mourning and other women will want what you have. This is your acceptable year. He will change the way you feel about everything you have gone through. God wants to comfort you and hold you close. You have fears, but He has comfort. Whatever you are dealing with, He has got the solution, and you will find it in His presence.

Restored and Made Whole!

God is ready to remove all your brokenness, to bring you out of captivity, and to give you a new garment to put on your life. The Bible calls it the garment of praise for the spirit of heaviness, that we might be called trees of righteousness, the planting of the Lord, that He might be glorified. God wants your life to glorify Him in the earthly realm. He came all the way to earth and sacrificed His life for you so that you could live with Him forever and become a carrier of His glory and of His presence. Genuine glory that begins on the inside of you and works its way out for others to see is supernatural: "Christ in you, the hope of realizing the glory". He is the real deal.

Restoring the Generations!

God's love is a miracle. When He says something to you, you can believe it, because He finishes what He starts. The Bible says, "They shall build the old wastes, they shall raise up the former desolation, and they shall repair the waste cities the desolations of many generations" (Isaiah 61:1-4, KJV). Not only will God repair and restore your life, but you will walk in such power that you will become the repairer of the breach. Yes, He will use you to help repair others' lives.

His Everlasting Arms

> The eternal God is my refuge, and underneath are the everlasting arms: and he shall thrust out the enemy from before thee; and shall say, Destroy them.
> —Deuteronomy 33:27 (KJV)

When you learn to lean in and abide in Him, you understand that underneath you are God's everlasting arms. When you walk in the door, the enemy runs and flees from you in terror because you carry His presence, and His arms are all around you. You watch as the work of your hands are established. His table will change the way you feel, the way you see things, and even change your heart. He will turn your mourning into dancing. Many times, you will commune with the Lord about something that will manifest shortly after your time with Him.

I remember a time when I was concerned about a problem I was facing. I sat in a chair and started talking to God about the situation, but before I had finished my time with Him, the phone rang, and the answer was there on the phone before we had finished our communion. He answered before I finished my time with Him. Yes, He is a very present help in your time of need.

Honor His Presence

As you enter in, be mindful of the Lord of hosts, let Him know you love Him, and remain grateful through constant surrender as He blesses your life. I remember returning to thank the Lord for even the simplest things that He did for me. My life was terribly busy as a young mother, but because my relationship with the Lord was so close, I would employ God's help wherever I needed it. I remember asking the Lord in periods of emergencies to help me wake up in the mornings. After a long day, I would be afraid of oversleeping, so at those times I got God involved. I would ask Him to wake me up on time, and without fail, He would. Whenever I looked at the clock, it was the exact time I had requested. No matter how often I asked, He did it every single time, but that's only the half of it, because not only did He wake me up on time, but I would awaken with no grogginess, feeling refreshed and praising God while preparing for my day. It was as if I had gotten a full eight hours of sleep instead of the three or four I actually received. I never forgot to honor Him. I always took time to turn to the Lord and say, "Thank You, Lord." I always knew God was there for me and my girls, helping me as I raised them. So, the least I could do was turn and thank Him.

Gratefulness Can Make You Whole

> And they lifted up their voices, and said, Jesus, Master, have mercy on us. And when he saw them, he said unto them, Go shew yourselves unto the priests. And it came to pass, that, as they went, they were cleansed. And one of them, when he saw that he was healed, turned back, and with a loud voice glorified God, And fell down on his face at his feet, giving him thanks: and he was a Samaritan. And Jesus answering said, Were there not ten cleansed? But where are the nine? There are not found that returned to give glory to God, save this stranger. And he said unto him, Arise, go thy way: thy faith hath made thee whole.
>
> —Luke 17:13-19 (KJV)

This man's thankfulness to God got him made whole that day. Too often, we are not grateful to God for the things He provides us, the things that He gives us, and even what He protects us from. We live thankless lives, always concentrating on the negative instead of the positive. So, your thankfulness, for starters, should begin with the fact that the Lord woke you up this morning. Everybody did not wake up this morning, but you did. So, can you give God glory for that? Just look around. What else can you find to give God glory for in your life?

I guess you get my point. This man turned back to thank God for healing him of his leprosy, and because of his thankful heart, Jesus released an additional blessing on the man, making him whole. That nose of his that had fallen off because of the leprosy was restored; he got a new nose. He became the blessed one that day. The others got cleansed, but he became whole. Thankfulness towards God pays off with rich dividends, but most of all, it develops the character of our souls and releases a sweet aroma back to God. Thanking God feels good.

My Declaration

With determined purpose, in everything, I will release thanksgiving and praise back to God.

IT'S TIME!

Ladies, thank you so much for completing this portion of the book. Your thirty-day "love calendar" challenge is just ahead. The first half of the book is designed to tenderize your heart while increasing your capacity and desire for more of God. The second half of the book is your awaiting challenge that will walk you step-by-step out of brokenness and into emotional wholeness. The challenge is a thirty-day adventure. Every day, something new will occur on your journey; something that you have not experienced before with the Lord. Each day will come with specific task that will heal the heart and prepare you for lasting love. So, enjoy this opportunity to get close to God, and allow Him to get closer to you than ever before. Remember, Jesus is knocking on the door of your heart, so do not allow His request to go unanswered.

Now, you may proceed to your thirty-day challenge by turning the page. However, be careful to read all instructions for the challenge and be sure to follow them exactly.

Karl and Toni Eubanks, Wedding Day, September 17, 2016

Me, My Huband, and Our Daughters

Me and My Mom

Toni Eubanks

The Thirty-Day Challenge Calendar

MEASURING YOUR HEART

To begin the challenge, we must first measure your emotional heart for healing.

Take out a pen and a notebook or some paper (if you don't want to fill in your answers in the book). Write down the answers to the questions below to help you gauge where you are today versus where you will be by the end of the challenge. Be honest with God—you have nothing to protect!

Honestly record what your life has manifested so far. Take a moment to reflect, then write your answers before you begin the calendar. After writing your answers, safely fold up that piece of paper, put it away, and do not go back to make changes or updates during the thirty-day calendar portion of the challenge.

1. How do you feel emotionally about your life now?

_____
_____
_____
_____
_____
_____
_____
_____
_____
_____

2. In what direction do you feel your life is headed?

3. Are you satisfied with your life, or are there places of regret that are hard to release?

4. How are your relationships currently, and where do you see your relationships headed?

5. How do you feel about your walk with the Lord, and are you happy with where you are with God?

6. Do you feel that your life is properly aligned with your purpose?

INTRODUCTION
to the Thirty-Day Challenge Calendar

Welcome to the "Challenge Adventure" calendar section of *The Thirty-Day Challenge to Connect and Fall in Love with the Man of Your Dreams*! The thirty-day challenge is a Bible-based and biblically sound supernatural healing tool. It includes thirty days of instructional tasks designed to help heal and free the emotional, hurting heart. It is based primarily upon the Song of Solomon as well as other key scriptures that work synergistically together to produce emotional healing.

The calendar has been structured and designed specifically to bring the emotional heart to a peaceful condition and to remove the barriers to real love in just thirty days. The previous chapters have been lessons to tenderize the heart, and the thirty-day calendar on the following pages is structured to reposition and prepare the freed heart, mind, and body for spiritual intimacy and natural love. It is your recipe for success. Daily calendar instructions are just ahead!

Let's Agree in Prayer for Your Thirty-Day Challenge Journey

Father, in the name of Jesus, I enter into agreement with the woman of God reading this challenge. She is now ready to begin her own adventure with You. So, Father, I ask that You remove every hinderance and break the power of every work of the enemy in her life, now, in Jesus' name. Draw her closer to You than she has ever been before. Allow her to feel Your gaze upon her. Father, reveal to her the destiny that You have designed for her; speak and confirm those mysteries into her heart that she needs to receive. Now, Father God, seal her by the power of the Holy Spirit, in Jesus' name. Afterwards, Father, make her able to walk through every situation that she faces in life with safety and ease. I thank You, Father, for the grace to do all that You have ordained for her to accomplish in the earthly realm, in the name of Jesus. Amen.

Special Instructions to Easily Follow the Challenge Calendar

Start each morning when you are fresh for best results, or in the evening when you are alone. You will only need obedience, your Bible, and your imagination.

Each day, follow and match the numbered picture below with that day's calendar task. Then, follow that day's instructions as written. You deserve an authentic experience with God, so do not look days ahead. Do not cheat yourself. This is your adventure and intimate time with Beloved.

Each day is filled with its own task and surprises. Whatever arrives that day, see yourself in that moment with it. Obey the task as they are written. Stay there in your mind and meditate on the experience for a time. Then, receive the encounter by faith as you look forward to the next day's encounter.

If you obey the instructions contained in these pages, by the end of the thirty days, you will be well on your way to emotional wholeness and you will be able to feel your wholeness rising inside you. You will also be able to utilize the spiritual tools acquired to face other challenges in life. So, remember to take each day one day at a time and do not look ahead. Again, do not cheat yourself. Let's get started; day one is just ahead.

The Challenge

The Thirty-Day Challenge to Connect and Fall in Love with the Man of Your Dreams   105

Day 1

No more excuses. Your past has hindered your future. See #33 below and read Song of Solomon 1:5-6 (KJV) and Hebrews 12:11-15 (KJV).

Now, reflect on how these scriptures apply to your own life.

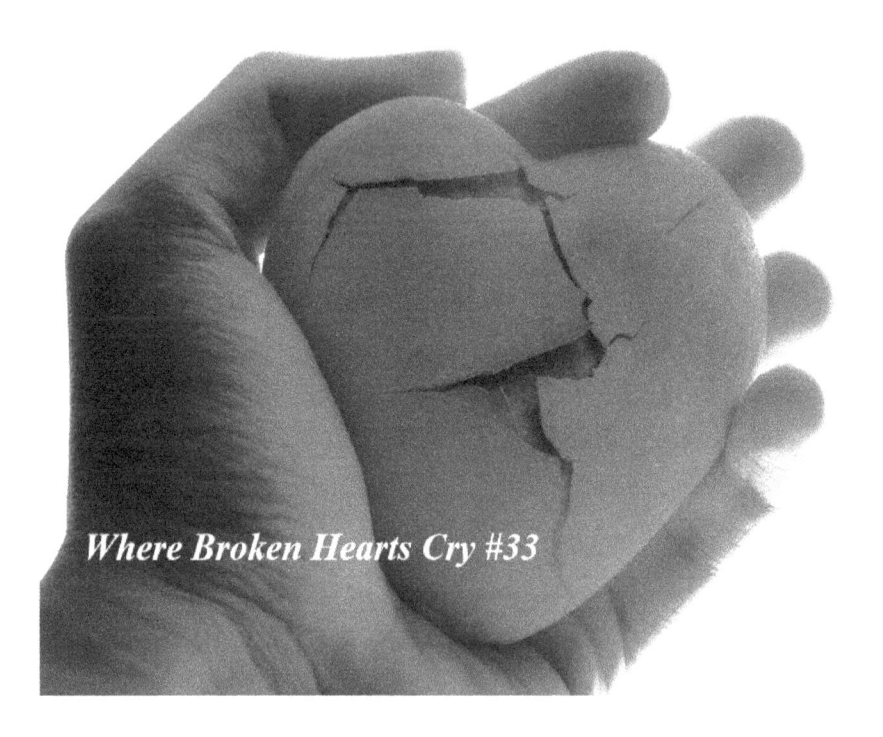

Where Broken Hearts Cry #33

DAY 1 REFLECTIONS

Day 2

The journey to wholeness takes time. With reckless abandonment, make a list of all who have hurt you, past and present. Name them. Include hurts from your family of origin, where you grew up. Also include romantic and social wounding. Talk to God about each case. Use an extra piece of paper if needed. There is nothing to protect.

LIST YOUR HURTS, PAST AND PRESENT

_____
_____
_____
_____
_____
_____
_____
_____
_____
_____
_____
_____
_____
_____
_____
_____
_____
_____

Day 3

Because there is no healing outside the cross, you must do #58. Use Mark 11:25-26 (KJV).

Apply it to old loves, family members, and those on your list from yesterday. Use the four parts to prayer below for each case today.

Discard Old Garments #58

This four-part prayer must be prayed out loud and applied individually to each case from yesterday's list. Read the four-part prayer below:

Prayer begins here for each case on your list.

PART 1: FORGIVE FIRST

> "Father God, I come to you now, in Jesus' name, and I bring to remembrance the time when (name the case/person/offense) hurt me by (recall out loud before the Father what happened). I choose to release what he/she/they did and/or said. I choose to forgive them now, according to Mark 11:25 and 26 (KJV). I stand praying before You now, and I choose to forgive as You commanded me. I release him/her/them and let him/her/them go, free of this offense right now, in Jesus' name. I give this offense to You, Father God, right now, in Jesus' name."

See yourself giving the offense to Jesus. Stay there in the moment for as long as you need to.

PART 2: RECEIVE YOUR OWN FORGIVENESS

"Now, Father God, I ask You to forgive me for the way my heart reacted to what was done to me. Forgive me for the sin of judgement that I made in my heart against them. I ask You to forgive me now, in Jesus' name, and I receive my own forgiveness right now, by faith in Jesus' name. Now, Father God, I uproot every bitterroot judgment planted in my heart by the enemy concerning that sin. I uproot it all now, in Jesus' name, and I take it all to the cross of Christ now, in the name of Jesus."

PART 3: GATHER YOUR FRAGMENTS AND TAKE EACH OF THEM TO THE CROSS

"Father God, I understand that the cross is the stopping place for all sin, for all pain, and for all death. Therefore, I thank You, Father, that all the sin committed against me by (name them here) is now put to death, right now at the cross, in Jesus' name. The judgment I made in my heart is also now uprooted concerning (name them here); I put it to death, right now, at the cross, in Jesus' name. Thank You, Father, that all of the power of that sin is put to death now, in Jesus' name. It all stops now: the raging, the pain, the hurt, and the sin; it all dies and is put to death, right now, at the cross where Jesus died for it, in Jesus' name. I have forgiven and I am forgiven. Thank You, Father; my heart is set free right now, in Jesus' name. Thank You, Jesus; the striving is gone and I am set free, in Jesus' name. Thank You, Jesus. Thank You, Jesus. Thank You, Jesus. I am set free, in Jesus' name."

PART 4: PRAISE AND RECEIVE YOUR RESURRECTION

"Thank You, Father God, that just as Jesus was resurrected on the third day, I receive my heart, resurrected to new life and new wholeness, in Jesus' name! Old things have passed away and all things are become new now in my life, in Jesus' name! Hallelujah! Hallelujah! Amen."

Celebrate your freedom from each case.

Day 4

So much awaits you. It is time to move forward. Pray for #45 and read Matthew 25:1-10 (KJV).

Develop & Increase Your Oil #45

DAY 4 REFLECTIONS

_____
_____
_____
_____
_____
_____
_____
_____
_____

Day 5

A gift has arrived: #9. Unwrap it by reading John 4:13-14 (KJV). Plans are in the making. Read Psalm 42:7-8 (KJV).

The Deepest Part Of Your Beloved #9

PRAYER TO RECEIVE THE BAPTISM OF THE HOLY SPIRIT:

Father God, I come before You in the name of Jesus. I believe that You are God and that You saved the world through Your Son, Jesus Christ. I accept Him as my Lord and my Savior. I know it is Your desire that I be comforted throughout my life in the earth and I receive You as the God of all comfort; the umpire of my soul and spirit. Lord, I ask that You fill me with Your precious Holy Spirit until I overflow with the evidence of His presence. By faith, I receive Your Holy Spirit right now into my life and into my heart, in Jesus' name. I receive the infilling of His holy presence by faith. Holy Spirit, breathe on me, rise up inside me. Lead me and guide me into all the truth, light my pathway before me, comfort me, and order my steps always. I receive You by faith today, in Jesus' name. Amen.

DAY 5 REFLECTIONS

Day 6

Someone has arrived, but you can only peep to see at #97 and at Song of Solomon 2:8-9 (KJV).

Your Beloved Has Arrived #97

WHAT ARE YOU FEELING AT THIS MOMENT?

_____
_____
_____
_____
_____
_____
_____
_____
_____
_____

Day 7

A picnic is planned, and #97 will be there. You will meet at #48. Do not be late.

Read Song of Solomon 1:2-4 (KJV) and Song of Solomon 2:1-3 (KJV).

You will find Him at the meeting place below.

Underneath The Apple Tree #48

WERE YOU ABLE TO SAVOR HIS PRESENCE?
HOW DID HIS FRUIT TASTE?

Day 8

Beloved has opened Himself to you. Meditate the wonders of His person at Psalm 24:1-10 (KJV), and Psalm 27:4-6 (KJV) then mull His longing embrace. Do #39.

Pause To Build A Memory #39

HOW DOES THE POWER OF HIS PRESENCE FEEL?

_____
_____
_____
_____
_____
_____
_____
_____

Day 9

You are accepted in the beloved. It is time to let Him know how you feel. Do #57. Then read it out loud to Him using the power of the spoken word.

Write your Beloved #57

IN WHAT WAY IS YOUR LOVE GROWING FOR HIM?

_____
_____
_____
_____
_____
_____
_____
_____
_____
_____

Day 10

Your letter pleased your Beloved. He sends the Key to your wholeness #55. Along with 5 Crucial Benefits Hidden Within Your Forgiveness. Use Proverbs 4:23 (KJV) and Zechariah 2:18(KJV) to absorb His goodness today.

The Power of Forgiveness #55

5 Crucial Benefits Hidden Within Your Forgiveness:

1. Your forgiveness is a weapon against the enemy of your soul that only you can wield.
2. Your forgiveness causes the transgressions of others to become your power to rise.
3. Your forgiveness renews the body to make you healthy, renewed, and whole.
4. Your forgiveness ushers in new seasons of goodness.
5. Your forgiveness will open to you pearls of new wisdom and understanding.

WHAT IS FORGIVENESS BEGINNING TO PRODUCE WITHIN YOU?

Day 11

An unexpected note has been placed under your door. See #68. Then, read it at John 14:1-3 (KJV) and at John 14:13-14 (KJV).

A love letter has arrived #68

Daily, He is loading you with benefits. In what ways can you sense them?

DAY 11 REFLECTIONS

_____
_____
_____
_____
_____

Day 12

You are falling in love. You revisit your special places with Him. See #39, then read Psalm 23:1-6 (KJV).

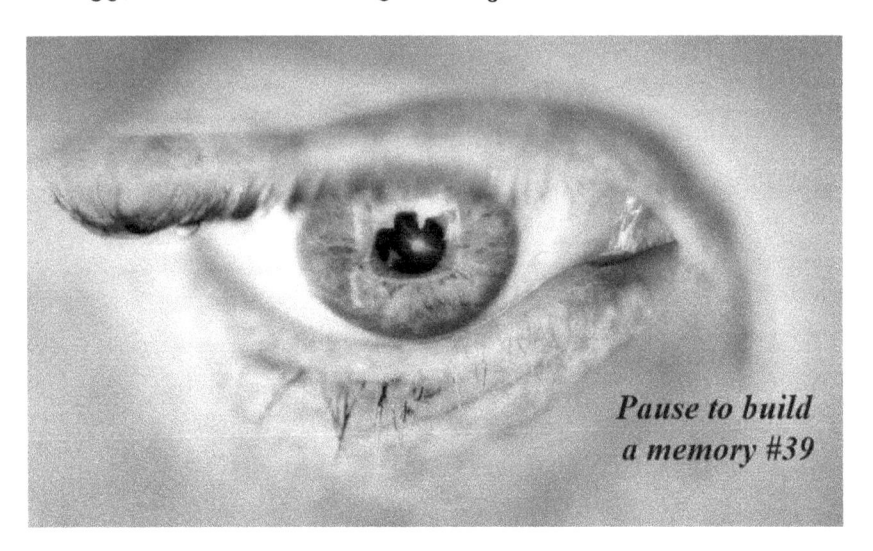

Pause to build a memory #39

IN WHAT WAY IS HE RESTORING YOU?

_____
_____
_____
_____
_____
_____
_____
_____
_____
_____
_____

Day 13

Your Beloved misses you. He has sent #69, along with Psalm 149: 3-4 (KJV) and Psalm 30:11-12 (KJV). Dance with Him in your heart all day there.

An invitation to dance #69

HOW DO YOU IMAGINE PRAISING HIM IN THE DANCE TO BE?

_____
_____
_____
_____
_____
_____
_____
_____

Day 14

You are overwhelmed with the extravagance of His love. You must respond with #64

The Power Of The Spoken Word #64

TELL HIM HOW YOU TRULY FEEL ABOUT HIM

_____
_____
_____
_____
_____
_____
_____
_____
_____

Day 15

More work is required in your heart. Read John 15:1-8 (KJV). Pray today to abide in Him.

IN WHAT WAYS WILL YOU CONTINUALLY ABIDE IN HIM?

Day 16

Beloved whispers His own desire in Isaiah 40:1-5 (KJV). He offers His own challenge at Matthew 8:20 (KJV) and at Matthew 22:33-40 (KJV).

Will you be His resting place?

HOW CAN BELOVED FIND REST IN YOU?

_____
_____
_____
_____
_____
_____
_____
_____
_____
_____
_____

Day 17

You miss your Beloved. Send #57 and read Psalm 42:1-7 (KJV). Worship Him while waiting for His response.

Write your Beloved #57

IN YOUR LONGINGS FOR HIM,
WHAT DO YOU WANT HIM TO KNOW?

_____
_____
_____
_____
_____
_____
_____
_____
_____

Day 18

Love will not be silent. A response has come; see #68.

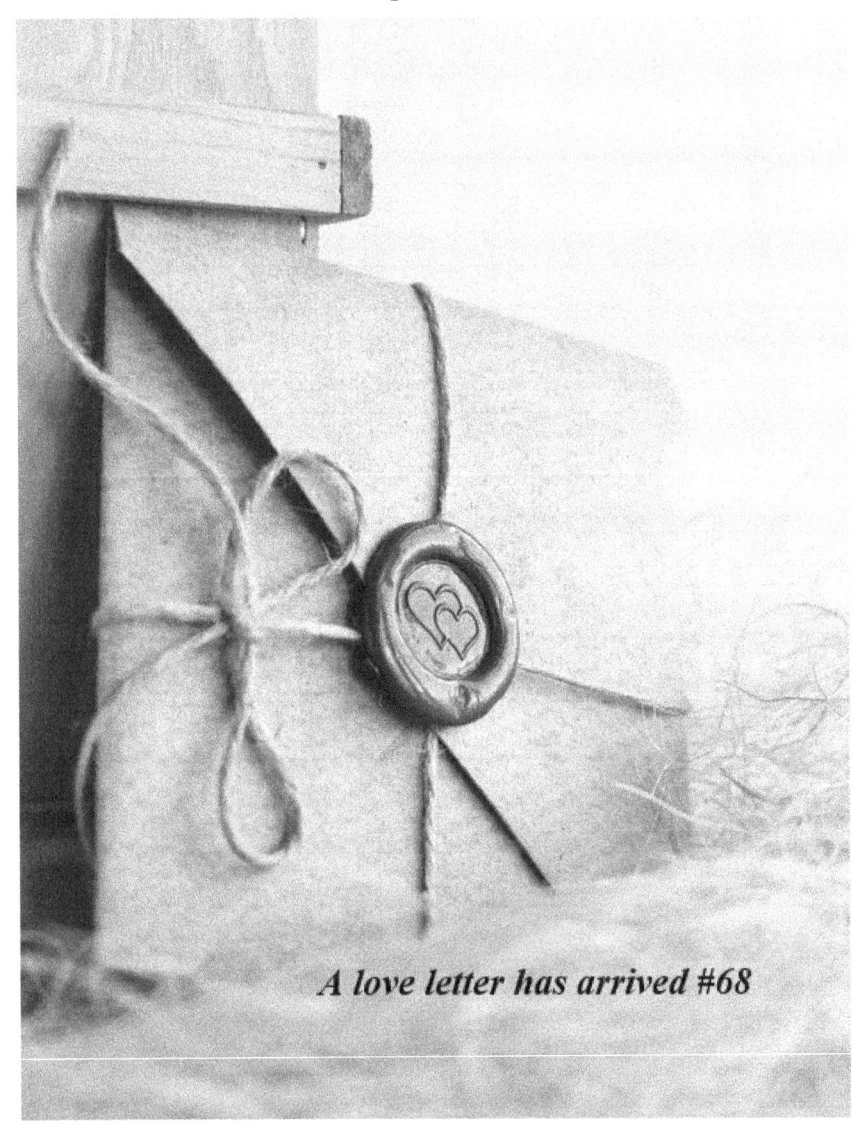

A love letter has arrived #68

Read His response at Song of Solomon 4:9-16 (KJV) and at John 16:24 (KJV).

Ask Him now for your heart's desire!

DAY 18 REFLECTIONS

Day 19

Beloved is requesting you at #48. Read Song of Solomon 2:5-6 (KJV). Be sure to build a memory.

Underneath the apple tree #48

IN WHAT WAYS DO YOU SENSE HIM EMBRACING YOU?

_____
_____
_____
_____
_____
_____
_____
_____
_____
_____
_____

Day 20

Beloved whispers #88. You will give Him your love today at Song of Solomon 7:10-13 (KJV) and at Matthew 11:28-30 (KJV).

Beloved assures you your love is safe with Him #88

WHAT NEW FRUIT ARE YOU DISCOVERING, AND IN WHAT WAY IS HIS BURDEN LIGHT?

_____
_____
_____
_____
_____
_____
_____

Day 21

You pleased your Beloved so much yesterday, He has sent #5, along with Isaiah 61:1-3 (KJV) and John 15:16 (KJV).

Beloved Sends Warmth #5

IN WHAT WAY DO HIS WORDS WARM YOU?

_____
_____
_____
_____
_____
_____
_____
_____
_____

Day 22

Beloved is securing you. Your faith is building in His love for you. You know you will never be the same. Use #64 to speak out loud your faith in His love.

YOUR DECLARATION

_____
_____
_____
_____
_____
_____
_____
_____
_____

Day 23

A very special delivery has come. Use #79 to see. Begin to prepare for the coming Banquet. Read Psalm 51:6-12 (KJV) and Proverbs 4:18-27 (KJV).

#79

IN WHAT WAYS ARE YOU PREPARING
FOR THE COMING BANQUET?

_____
_____
_____
_____
_____
_____
_____
_____

Day 24

Enlarge your heart and increase your oil #45. Endeavor to make this anticipated encounter beautiful.

Develop & Increase Your Oil #45

HOW WILL YOU INCREASE YOUR OIL TODAY?

_____
_____
_____
_____
_____
_____
_____
_____
_____
_____
_____
_____

Day 25

Beloved adores you. He is mindful of your efforts. He sends you balm from Gilead to restore you #85 along with Proverbs 4:20-22 (KJV) and Song of Solomon 6:4-10 (KJV).

Balm from Gilead   #85

Beloved is the only healing salve you'll ever need. When you have time today, close your eyes for a few minutes and in the spirit of your mind see and feel the spiritual balm of His words covering every area of your heart.

DAY 25 REFLECTIONS

Day 26

Surprise! Beloved has shopped for you. To accept His new garment, you must shake off the old ways of doing things.

Read Isaiah 52: 1-3 (KJV).

Now, accept His gift. Try it on in mind, then go to the mirror at Isaiah 61:10-11 (AMPC) to see your reflection.

> I will greatly rejoice in the Lord, my soul shall exult in my God; for He has clothed me with the garments of salvation, He has covered me with the robe of righteousness, as a bridegroom decks himself with a garland, and as a bride adorns herself with her jewels. For as [surely as] the earth brings forth its shoots, and as a garden causes what is sown in it to spring forth, so [surely] the Lord God will cause rightness and justice and praise to spring forth before all the nations [through the self-fulfilling power of His word].
>
> —Isaiah 61:10-11 (AMPC)

The Thirty-Day Challenge to Connect and Fall in Love with the Man of Your Dreams

Day 27

Last-minute fragments must be gathered. Check your heart for any remnants of unforgiveness. See #58.

Releasing the past opens the door to His abundance #58

Is there anyone left out that still needs to be forgiven or to be released in prayer? Take the time to use the four-part prayer guide for all remaining fragments.

DAY 27 REFLECTIONS

_____
_____
_____
_____
_____
_____
_____
_____

Day 28

Your hard work has paid off. You have made yourself ready. Beloved's glow is growing and increasing inside you. You are prepared.

Read Isaiah 60:1-5 (KJV) and Isaiah 43:18-21 (KJV). Reflect your journey.

DAY 28 REFLECTIONS

Day 29

Banquet day has arrived. With heart wide open, go to meet #97 at Jeremiah 31:11-14 (KJV) and at Song of Solomon 2:1-17 (KJV).

REMINISCE ON ALL THAT WAS DONE TO MAKE THIS DAY POSSIBLE.

_____
_____
_____
_____
_____
_____
_____
_____
_____
_____

Day 30

Love has changed you. #97 whispers John 14:18 (KJV), Song of Solomon 4:7-16 (KJV) and Isaiah 41:10-13 (KJV). With great pride, Beloved places His eternal signet below on your heart forever.

Beloved offers you His eternal signet, precious jewels, and His promises. He vows to make you a sign and a wonder in the earth.

Read Isaiah 62:1-12.

Openly declare your commitment to the Lord your Beloved by praying the prayer below out loud:

> "Lord Jesus, I stand/kneel before You this day. I know You as my Savior and I now take You as the Lover of my soul, here and now. I receive Your eternal seal upon my heart, forever and always. Now, Lord, I forgive everyone who has hurt and wounded me from my past. I will no longer hold on to what happened. I release them all. I release all judgements, hurt, and unforgiveness I made in my heart against them. Now, Lord Jesus, I gather all those fragments, all the hurts, the wounds, and all the bitterroot judgements from my past. I gather them up and I take them all to the cross, the place of death, and I put them all to death at the cross now, in Jesus' name. I see them all nailed there at the cross, in Jesus' name. All the anger, resentment, and every emotional wound is put to death there now, in Jesus' name. Thank You, Lord Jesus, that it all stops at the cross. All the hurt and pain of my past, it all stops now at the cross, in Jesus' name. Thank You, Jesus. Thank You for healing my heart, my soul, and my emotions right now, in Jesus' name. I receive Your healing balm, covering me and saturating my being now, in Jesus' name. I receive Your resurrection power, Lord Jesus, bringing me back to life in hidden areas. Thank You, Jesus. I am accepted in the Beloved, in the name of Jesus. I am joined and fastened to You and I receive the eternal seal of Your Holy Spirit upon my heart. I open my heart to the adventures of the Holy Spirit and the whispers of God. I receive Your calling and your desire for my life. Thank You that Your banner of love is waving over my life and over my family. I commit to live a life of forgiveness

and wholeness; where you lead, I will follow. Now, Lord Jesus, propel me into the destiny You have planned for my life, right now, in Jesus' name. Amen."

Your New Beginning Starts Here!

TO COMPLETE YOUR ENCOUNTER, WE MUST MEASURE YOUR RESULTS.

It is time to write about your experiences during the challenge and how it has changed your life these past thirty days. Take out a pen and paper again and carefully record how you truly feel as a result of having read and completed *The Thirty-Day Challenge to Connect and Fall in Love with the Man of Your Dreams* by answering the following questions:

1. How do you now feel spiritually after completing the challenge?

_____
_____
_____
_____
_____
_____
_____
_____
_____
_____
_____
_____
_____
_____
_____
_____

2. What, if anything, has changed within, and can you feel your wholeness rising inside you?

3. How has your relationship with God changed?

4. How are you emotionally now, and were you able to uproot hurts and wounds from your past?

5. In what way has your outlook on your life changed after completing the challenge?

6. Has your life healed, and if so, in what ways?

7. What do you understand the tools to keep your family members emotionally whole and secure to be?

8. In what ways do you feel more aligned with God's purposes for your life?

9. How, if at all, has your physical body been impacted after completing the challenge?

After completing the information above, put away what you have written and come back in 24 hours to measure your results.

TWENTY-FOUR HOURS LATER

Take out the information and details written yesterday along with the information and details written before you began the challenge. Now, first read the details you wrote at the beginning before you began the thirty day challenge. Take a moment to reflect on what was written. Take deep breaths if you need to, then begin again when you are ready.

After reading the first details, now open and read the details and information you wrote yesterday after completing the thirty day challenge. Take a moment and meditate the difference you feel after having taken the challenge. Be sure to meditate your new love relationship with the Lord, His goodness, as well as your newfound closeness with Him. You have the tools to keep His love, peace, and wholeness flowing in your life continually, and you will never be the same. Begin releasing thanksgiving and praise to the Lord for how He has transformed your life and made you whole in just thirty days.

SPECIAL BLESSINGS

Women that are whole draw men that are whole to them. They are not afraid to walk away from the enemies table. They are secure and thoroughly furnished by Him alone. They safely abide in that special place with Him as He watches and cares for them. Their emotional wholeness will draw healthy relationships and also strengthen them to walk away from toxic situations and men that treat them badly. They simply lose their taste for that which is not from God. They live in joy and expectancy underneath His everlasting arms and God makes His plans their reality.

TESTIMONIES OF HEALING

Send testimonies of healing to: 30days2lovechallenge@gmail.com

SPREAD THE HEALING

The Thirty-Day Challenge to Connect and Fall in Love with the Man of Your Dreams is the best gift you can give to a woman who is hurting.

Sow a seed of healing by purchasing a copy of this book, then plant it in someone's life today.

PRAYER OF SALVATION

Accepting Christ as your Lord and Savior changes you forever. Below is a prayer to do just that, right here, right now.

"Heavenly Father, I come to You now and I ask You to forgive me for all my sins. I confess with my mouth and I believe with my heart that Jesus Christ is Your Son. I believe that He died on the cross at Calvary for all mankind and that He died for me as well so that I might be forgiven and receive eternal life in Your kingdom. Father, I believe that Jesus was crucified for me and that You, Father God, rose Him from the dead for me as You said in Your Word. You said, Father God, that if I would believe with my heart and confess with my mouth that Jesus is Lord and accept Him as my Lord and Savior, then I would be saved. Therefore, Father, I repent of all my sins and I receive You now, Lord Jesus, as my Lord and Savior. I ask You to save me right now. I receive my salvation right now, in Jesus' name. I will worship You, Lord Jesus, all the days of my life! Thank You, Lord, that Your Word is true. Salvation is eternally sealed in Christ in God. I am a child of God now and I have been transferred from eternal death to eternal life. I belong to You, Lord Jesus, for now and forever. Thank You, Lord, for what You did for me at Calvary. Thank You, Lord, for saving me. I am saved, now and forever. Amen."

That if thou shalt confess with thy mouth the Lord

Jesus, and shalt believe in thine heart that God hath raised him from the dead, thou shalt be saved. For with the heart man believeth unto righteousness; and with the mouth confession is made unto salvation.

Romans 10:9-10 (KJV)

ABOUT THE AUTHOR

Toni Eubanks is a woman who wears many hats. She is a wife, mother, counselor, minister, and life coach. Toni was raised in Birmingham, Alabama, U.S.A. and has been leading women into emotional wholeness ever since she received her own inner healing nearly thirty years ago. Toni is a born-again believer in Christ. Through her ministry, Healing Fire, she has led thousands of women into wholeness and into the blessings that a lifestyle of wholeness brings. Toni's step-by-step healing processes are based on the Word of God and have been administered to women through meetings, seminars, conferences, and online. Women report amazing transformations and lasting results. Women also discover permanent tools and healing processes to lead their own family members into a lifestyle of wholeness. Because Toni has expanded her emotional healing ministry to reach more hurting women, *The Thirty-Day Challenge to Connect and Fall in Love with the Man of Your Dreams* message is now available in book form for women of God worldwide. The thirty-day challenge is for women of God who are ready to heal their lives and live within the best version of themselves. The thirty-day challenge provides the unique opportunity for women of God to heal in privacy in just thirty days.

SCRIPTURE APPENDIX

1. Proverbs 10:22 (KJV)
2. Matthew 22: 2-14 (KJV)
3. Jeremiah 29:11 (AMPC)
4. Jeremiah 29:11 (NIV)
5. Jeremiah 29:12 (AMPC)
6. Song of Solomon 2:4 (AMPC)
7. Colossians 1:27 (KJV)
8. Psalms 16:11 (KJV)
9. Acts 2:25 (KJV)
10. Revelations 3:20 (AMPC)
11. Proverbs 31:10-11 (KJV)
12. Proverbs 31:15 (AMPC)
13. Proverbs 31:30 (AMPC)
14. John 17:17 (KJV)
15. Ephesians 6:15 (KJV)
16. Song of Solomon 1:6 (KJV)
17. Jeremiah 29:12-14 (AMPC)
18. 1 Cor. 7:34 (KJV)
19. Psalm 19:9-10 (KJV)
20. Psalm 16:11 (KJV)
21. John 14:18 (KJV)
22. Matthew 11:28-30 (KJV)
23. Matthew 9:20-22 (KJV)
24. Matthew 11:12 (AMPC)
25. Luke 10:40-41 (KJV)

26. John 15:3 (KJV)
27. John 15:5 (KJV)
28. John 15: 4-5 (KJV)
29. Song of Solomon 1:5-6 (KJV)
30. Proverbs 20:27 (KJV)
31. Luke 15:11-24 (KJV)
32. 2 Samuel 4:4 (KJV)
33. 2 Samuel 9:1 (KJV)
34. Hebrews 12:11-15 (KJV)
35. Song of Solomon 1:2-4 (KJV)
36. Jeremiah 8:22 (KJV)
37. Luke 7: 37-48 (KJV)
38. Matthew 25:1-13 (KJV)
39. Matthew 25:9 (KJV)
40. Philippians 3:10 (KJV)
41. Philippians 3:10 (AMPC)
42. Isaiah 61: 1-4 (KJV)
43. Deuteronomy 33:27 (KJV)
44. Luke 17:13-19 (KJV)
45. Psalm 105: 8-21 (KJV)
46. 1 Corinthians 13:7-8 (AMPC)

CPSIA information can be obtained
at www.ICGtesting.com
Printed in the USA
FSHW020303030521
80960FS